CHEIKH ANTA DIOP

AN INTELLECTUAL PORTRAIT

*Baba Emory
In Victory
Molefi K Asante
2-23-07*

CHEIKH ANTA DIOP

AN INTELLECTUAL PORTRAIT

MOLEFI KETE ASANTE

University of Sankore Press

Los Angeles

2007

UNIVERSITY
OF
SANKORE
PRESS

Sankore

Cheikh Anta Diop: An Intellectual Portrait
© 2007 by University of Sankore Press

Graphic Design:
University of Sankore Press Collaborative

Front Cover Hieroglyphs Translation:
"Speak truth; do justice, for it is mighty" from the Book of Khunanpu, *The Husia*

International Standard Book Number: 978-0-943412-26-9

Library of Congress Cataloging-in-Publication Data

Asante, Molefi K., 1942–
    Cheikh Anta Diop: an intellectual portrait / Molefi Kete Asante—1st ed.
        p. cm.
    Includes bibliographical references and index.
    ISBN-13: 978-0-943412-26-9
    1. Diop, Cheikh Anta. 2. Diop, Cheikh Anta—Political and social views. 3. Historians—Senegal—Biography. 4. Intellectuals—Senegal—Biography. 5. Africa—Historiography. 6. Blacks—Historiography. I. Title.
    DT19.7.D56A83 2006
    960.072'02—dc22
                                                2006027330

CONTENTS

CONTENTS

ACKNOWLEDGEMENTS

I would like to express my sincere gratitude to those who have listened to me over the years as I decried the fact that we had no introductory work on Cheikh Anta Diop in English. A number of works have been produced in French by scholars who are attempting to follow in Diop's path. Cheikh's own son, Cheikh M'Backe Diop has produced a very useful account of his father's life and work. I acknowledge Cheikh M'Backe for his friendship and generosity. There is in Paris a remarkable group of intellectuals, for the most part professionals in science, who have taken on the work of Cheikh Anta Diop.

I want to personally acknowledge all of the scholars I have read with benefit believing that any book on Diop would have to be influenced by the many things said about him, factual and legendary. I have tried to sift the information I have read and obtained from interviews and casual conversation with both scholars and everyday persons who knew and admired Diop.

Maulana Karenga, my brother, friend and colleague, has engaged in valuable dialog with me on the works of Diop and numerous other intellectual initiatives for victory over ignorance, falsification and dislocation. To him, I am thankful for his intellectual leadership.

People always ask me, how long did it take you to write a book? It is hard to say how long a work will take, some take ten years, others are ready in one year; this one has taken a lifetime because the distillation of Diop's thought into an easily readable volume is almost a magical act. If you are not a magician, and I am not, it is difficult to decide how to organize an individual's massive work into an introductory volume. All the failures of this introduction to the ideas of this great intellectual are mine.

I acknowledge all the people to whom I have not returned phone calls or emails. You know, I hope by now, that I was deeply involved in trying to get this work out. I want to personally acknowledge President Abdoulaye Wade of Senegal and President Thabo Mbeki of South Africa who both encouraged me to publish more works of this kind. My friend and brother, Cheikh Tidiane Gadio, Senior Minister for Foreign Affairs, Senegal, has been extremely helpful in getting me access to people, including President Wade, who knew the political climate in Senegal at the time of Cheikh Anta Diop's life. I am grateful to Ambassador Amadou Bocoum (Senegal's ambassador to India) for introducing me to Dame Tabou, a political associate of Cheikh Anta Diop. Ama Mazama, my colleague at Temple University, has been a steady and committed scholar, reading documents in French and directing me to sources that I would have never found on my own. I am also grateful to Haki Madhubuti, Safisha Madhubuti, Walter Lomax and Beverly Lomax for the discussions at *Abacus*.

Most of all, I acknowledge my wife, Ana Yenenga, whose critical eye, calm disposition, temperament of victory, constant love, humor, and great good common sense make my writing and teaching joyful and productive.

—MOLEFI KETE ASANTE
PHILADELPHIA

PREFACE

One day in the summer of 2002 when I was in Paris I went to Rue des Éoles and stared up at the apartment where Cheikh Anta Diop had lived during the time he was a student in Paris. I searched it up and down, looking for some sign that the great scholar had lived in the building. There was a historical marker on the building indicating that the Senegalese scholar had lived in the apartment during his college days. It was a clear victory for Africans in Paris who had campaigned to have the historical marker placed on the building, but there it was in Paris, an announcement that the great African scholar once lived in that building. I later went with Theophile Obenga, Ana Yenenga, Cheikh M'Backe, Diop's son, a nuclear physicist, to the small restaurant Café Perignon where Diop had his coffee and *du pain*.

To my amazement, Diop was present as if he had not died in February, 1986, because all we could talk about during our lunch was the presence of Diop and in a perfectly good African way we understood the eternal presence of a great ancestor. There was no budding hagiography here, only the concrete recognition that where we were was the exact place where Cheikh had often sat during his sojourn in Paris, a long ways from the sandy village of Caytou in the interior of Senegal.

Surrounded by the elements that were familiar to Cheikh Anta Diop we ate our food, drank our wine, something Cheikh would not have done, and had our cheese with a cup of coffee, while all the time commenting on the incredible obstacles Diop must have faced in adjusting to the anomie, individualism and alienation he saw around him in Paris. Was it here at Café Perignon where he got his major ideas for re-writing, indeed, in re-envisioning African history?

Upon reflection I could see that the resistance to the historical marker for Diop had been a part of the concerted effort to prevent Cheikh Anta Diop from occupying his proper place as an intellectual presence in our world. Actually, this effort had continued long after his death. Diop engaged in study, dedication, and intense struggle for truth that emerged as the inherited task of those who understand the awesome change that he single-handedly created in the academic world. What could prevent the Western world from considering him as one of the most significant thinkers of his time? It was a mixture of petty jealousies, intellectual insecurities, and the fear of losing a hegemonic hold on Africans that caused such animosity toward this important scholar. It would have been one thing had the critics of Diop confronted him on the arguments. But it was another thing to attack him personally, morally, or on the basis of some political agenda.

Thus, I have written this book not so much as a vindication of the man, because I am not a worshipper, but as a small introduction to Cheikh Anta Diop's intellectual gifts. I have left out some of the more abstract and dense intellectual works of Diop, believing that those interested in further study of his linguistic works will pursue other paths to do so. Therefore, the numerous scientific papers dealing with specific comparative linguistics have not been engaged in this work. Neither have I spent as much time as some future scholar should spend on Diop's political writings which are considerable. On the other hand, it was my purpose in this book to make Cheikh Anta Diop accessible to general as well as academic audiences.

In the course of many years of research on Cheikh Anta Diop I have talked to many scholars, gaining from them their special insights. I have spoken to Diop's family members and friends with equal benefit. My aim was to gather as much personal wisdom and knowledge as possible from those who knew him best. It was with this intention that I probed the mind of Theophile Obenga.

There have been many meetings between Obenga and myself, in Luxor, in Aswan at Elephantine, in Philadelphia, in Dakar, in Addis Ababa, in Hamburg, in Paris, and other places, and always I have been interested in knowing from him something of the personal Diop. He has not failed me in making his assessment.

"Cheikh Anta was a dedicated scientist," Obenga told me walk- ing across the Eastern desert where we had stopped en route to Abu Simbel where he started a tradition of calling upon Ramses II, *setep en Re*, and responding to his stone presence with the understanding that we are the children of Ramses. But I wanted more about Diop, the man who had designated Obenga as his heir in the struggle to put aright the history of the intellectual history of the African world.

What kind of man was Cheikh Anta Diop? From Obenga I learned that when Cheikh Anta Diop was in conference he was a powerful presence but that when he was finished with the meetings he went to his hotel to study and to rest. He was not a party goer and did not engage in the usual business of socializing after work. For him, life was dedicated to the mission of overturning the cruel hoax played on the African people by the falsifiers of our history. Meeting Diop in 1980 at IFAN near the campus of the University of Dakar, I cannot recall anything that struck me as insincere. He was straightforward, direct, humorous, and yet one could see in his willingness to talk about his work, the great joy he had in destroying the iconography of racism.

Cheikh Anta Diop understood the importance of a new conception of historiography in order to advance a more effective interpretation of African history. European authors created a problem in the interpretation of African history by seeking to impose their own ethnocentric biases onto the discovery of African reality. They wanted to speak for Africa rather than allow Africa to speak for itself. The historiography of Europe's writers was, like other concepts emerging out of a framework of the doctrine of White supremacy, racist. Looking for evidence of documents in Africa, Western writers declared Africans to be without history or as Hegel puts it, outside of history, because they could not find any histories written in Latin, Greek, or Hebrew. Their positioning of writing as a key factor in civilization was meant to reinforce European notions of superiority. Nevertheless, when it was discovered that there was more writing in ancient Africa than in Greece and Rome combined, the Westerners developed a strategy of marginalizing Africa. Also, it was argued that Egypt is not important and that it was a static society in contrast to Greece which was most important and dynamic. Diop smashed these ethnocentric constructions of historiography and history and reasserted the significance of Egypt, the whole of Africa and African agency by examining all aspects of the cultural life of Africa for clues to important puzzles and paradigms of human thought and practice.

If written documents were one source, then there was a whole host of sources that were unwritten: linguistics, oral narratives, art forms, physical texts, ethnology, musicology, burial customs, numismatics, etc. Few historians had ever used as many forms of evidence as Cheikh Anta Diop in establishing his principal theses.

Diop's arguments in support of the antiquity and achievements of ancient Kemet were based on the soundest of evidence and the most profound commentaries of the 20th century. In fact, he was a child of his century, utilizing all of the knowledge accumulated about ancient Africa during his time. The record was immense. Other authors have found similar evidence of Kemet's awesome achievements. As early as 1925, Walter Addison Jayne (1924:4) wrote that "The ancient Egyptians were a people of superior attainments. The conditions in the Nile valley being favorable to life and conducive to prosperity, the people utilized their advantages, developed their resources, and were pioneers and leaders in the arts of civilization". Jayne was a medical doctor who had reviewed the history of medicine in the world and concluded that Egypt in Africa was at the vanguard of civilization. Jayne was joined in his opinion by Elie Faure (1973:76) who said that the Greeks came to drink at the spring of Egypt. Clearly people came to Africa because the Egyptians excelled in the arts and sciences and were considered the wisest of all humans. Egypt dazzled a varied assortment of writers, artists, and scientists who entered its realm. Visitors also marveled at the wonders extending the length of the Nile in the country. Basil Davidson (1973:33), the famous popular historian, writes that the Greeks who saw their own country in its decline "had no difficulty in recognizing Egypt's greatness and accepting it as, in more ways than one, the master of their own civilization".

It is in this regard, that the Guyanese writer, George G. M. James (1954), felt so strongly about reappropriating what he called ancient Egypt's *Stolen Legacy*. James argued that much of what was claimed for Greece had roots in ancient Egyptian civilization and should be recognized as such. Diop, following a similar understanding, contended that the West had appropriated history by writing Africa out of it and by insisting that the Greeks had appeared with their own brand of wisdom totally fresh and original. If the omission was unintentional, one had to forget what one knew to come up with such fanciful notions. If the omission was deliberate and intentional, then it was one of the greatest acts of falsification in history and Cheikh Anta Diop was right to condemn it. He had legitimate grounds for claiming that the Western writers took Africa out of the equation of human history through a deliberate process of falsification. In the first place, they put forth false information. Secondly, they knew enough of the correct information because Europeans had gathered some of it. Finally, they were attempting to promote a racial supremacy position to accompany their geopolitical position. Also, one cannot dismiss the fact that the highest institutions of learning in the West participated in this cruel hoax on the people. Therefore, Diop understood that our central task would be to uncover the truth about Africa in all the disciplines of human knowledge.

Diop argued that there is strong evidence that philosophy began in Egypt. It is Diop's (1981:388; 1993:310) contention that philosophy in Kemet evolved as cosmogony as attested in the Pyramid Texts," in an epoch in which the Greeks themselves did not yet exist in history and in which the notions of a Chinese or Hindu philosophy had no meaning". Moreover, Will Durant (1954:193) says in the *Story of Civilization*, "Historians of philosophy have been wont to begin their story with the Greeks. The Hindus, who believe that they invented philosophy, and the Chinese, who believe that they perfected it, smile at our provincialism. It may be that we are all mistaken; for among the most ancient fragments left to us by Egyptians are writings that belong under the rubric of moral philosophy". What Durant goes on to say is that *The Teachings of Ptahhotep* is the oldest of all philosophy works, going back to 2800 B.C. However, Ptahhotep's writings are probably close to the same period of time as the now extinct work of Imhotep, the builder of the first pyramid and vizier of King Zoser. Nevertheless, whether we take Imhotep or Ptahhotep, these philosophers lived nearly 2300 years before Confucius, Socrates or Buddha. Ptahhotep, the governor of Memphis, and Prime Minister to the King, was like the philosopher who lived before him, Imhotep, dedicated to the transmission of moral wisdom and moral insight into building a Maatian or good society.

The Greeks were the children of the Egyptians. Mariette writes (Brodrick, 1892:xxxi) that Plato tells a story of Solon's visit to Egypt. Apparently, the priests of Sais said to him, "O Solon, Solon! You Greeks, you are nothing but children, there is not one old man among you in all Greece!" Among the Greeks who studied in Egypt were Thales, Solon, Pythagoras, Democritus of Abdera, Anaximander, Anaxigoras, Isocrates, and Plato (Granville, 1942:64–65). Diodorus Siculus (Oldfather, 1933–1967:90–91) puts it this way, "the Egyptians . . . were also greatly admired by the Greeks. For this reason, Greeks of the highest repute for learning were eager to visit Egypt, that they might gain knowledge of its noteworthy laws and customs . . . in ancient times Orpheus and the poet Homer were anxious to voyage thither, as were many others as well in later days, including Pythagoras of Samos and even Solon the lawgiver". Egypt embodied all wisdom and knowledge to the ancient Greeks who considered Egyptians the repositories of all philosophy.

Egypt was not only a superior civilization in philosophy but also in medicine. John A. Wilson contends that "there is a tradition that Egyptian physicians were in great demand in other countries, traveling to Asia Minor and Persia to practice their superior medical lore" (Breasted, 1930, I:17f). Of course, it was well known that the Egyptians had a great reputation for all their medical knowledge. Homer says in the Odyssey that the Egyptian physicians were skilled beyond all others, having among them specialists in particular branches of knowledge. When the Egyptians began to write about medicine their knowledge had already been old, so old in fact that some attributed it to the gods. All the physicians were priests, and the gods seemed to have been ever present.

In 1980, when I met Cheikh Anta Diop at his office at the Radio-carbon Laboratory of the Fundamental Institute of Black Africa, I was in Dakar attending the meeting held by Pathe Diagne on the possibility of repeating the Festival of the African World that had been held in Lagos, Nigeria in 1977. There were many scholars at this meeting. I was stunned to find as we assembled that Diop was not among the people who had been brought to the University. He was still considered an outsider to those in the elite groups of Senegal. But as the conference proceeded I broke away and found my way to IFAN, his office, just to pay respects and honor the great work that Diop had done for African people. He was warm, gracious, unassuming, and never flaunted his intellect nor his stature in the Black world. I found him to be a modest man of extraordinary talent; this was the real Cheikh Anta Diop whom we appreciated as an Imhotepian giant.

Purists might reproach me for not discussing all of the works of Diop in this book but I hope that the reader, with Ananse's generosity, will appreciate my attempt to make Diop's ideas understandable to the undergraduate as well as the graduate student, the scholar as well as the ordinary reader. Since Dr. Diop was a historian, physicist, sociologist, and linguist, he was comfortable in many intellectual traditions and methods. I am not attempting to trace every inch of his intellectual movement but rather to give the reader an appreciation for the broadest ideas in Diop's thinking while pointing out his most strident challengers and their challenges.

CHAPTER 1

CHEIKH ANTA DIOP'S LIFE AND TIMES

THE MAKING OF THE MAN

Cheikh Anta Diop was born in Caytou, near Diourbel, in Senegal in December, 1923 when Senegal was still a French colony. The title "Cheikh" was given to establish him as a legitimate heir to the great tradition of Islamic scholarship and intellectual erudition that had emerged among the Mourides. Nearly the entire continent of Africa, with the exception of Ethiopia and Liberia, was in the grip of a fierce European colonization. Resistance had been suppressed and the progressive forces were waiting for another good day to begin the push for the removal of the colonial forces. But for the moment, during the harmattan of 1923, one could hear only the voice of an infant crying in the night, a sign of the arrival of a disturber of the hegemonic "peace" that had been established by Western scholars.

In Europe, Germany had been defeated in the first great international war of Europe and France was in ascendancy. Perhaps some French even dreamed of the period of Napoleonic glory. Nothing seemed to stop French arrogance in its conquest of African territory. Having defeated the forces of Lat Dior and pushed through the railroad from Senegal to Mali, the French had connected two parts of its vast African holdings. Soon after the birth of Cheikh Anta Diop, the suppressed spirit of the people, despite the efforts of the French to split off Blaise Diagne, became another season of underground resistance by the Mourides brotherhood.

Diop was descended from a famous and important Mourides family. His grandfather, Mor Samba Diop, was the leading imam of the region, and an opponent of French colonialism. His father, Massamba Sassoum, died when he was very young and it was his formidable mother, Magatte Diop, who had a major role in shaping his early life. She was a brilliant woman, gifted with intelligence, integrity, and political *savoir-faire*. She sent her son to school in the city of Diourbel. He spent considerable time learning from the learned men of the Mourides order of Islam. This was the tradition of his family. He would travel in the company of his grandfather between Diourbel and the holy city of Touba in the Senegalese inte-rior. Having personally traveled that road I know that the journey must have been considerable in the days of Diop's youth. Neverthe-less, Touba was for all practical and religious purposes equal to any city in the world as a center for debate, scholarship, and high learn-ing. Cheikh Anta Diop became one of the scions of this tradition.

There was in Senegal, among the Mourides elite at the time, a strong educational culture and the young men who participated in it were some of the most noble in Senegalese history. Among the youth of Cheikh Anta Diop's day was Cheikh Sérigne M'Backe, the grandson of Cheikh Amadou Bamba, founder of the Mourides. M'Backe was also the inheritor of the leadership of the Mourides. Known for his erudition, scholarship, and openness to new ideas, Cheikh Sérigne M'Backe, who died in 1978, had been a long time friend to his cousin, Cheikh Anta Diop, who would live until 1986. Although their paths diverged in terms of the religious tradition they would always be friends, arguing over the political and social issues of the day. The younger Cheikh Anta admired the political skill and religious acumen of his older cousin yet he was never to become an imam or spiritual leader of Islam himself. He would, because of his outlook on life, become a devoted follower of science and inquiry.

Cheikh Anta Diop also attended school with Mor Sourang, son of a wealthy businessman, and Doudou Thiam, who became the head of Senegalese diplomacy. Both were long time acquaintances who can be said to have had an impact on the quickness of the young Diop's mind. Mor Sourang served the political establishment with his brilliant construction of diplomatic positions in the interest of the country.

The relationship between Cheikh Anta Diop and the young Cheikh Sérigne M'Backe was one of close friendship and fraternity. Cheikh M'Backe was descended through his mother from Lat Dior Ngone Latyr Diop, who was the last Damel of Cayor, that is, the last of the emperors of the Wolof Empire. He had fought the French to his death. According to Pathe Diagne (2002:11), the nickname for Cheikh M'Backe was "The Lion of Fatma." In fact, Cheikh Anta Diop was to name one of his children after M'Backe. Diagne believes that this was a formative relationship for Diop. Indeed, if one looks at the evidence it seems that the older Cheikh M'Backe was a key influence on the developing philosophy of Cheikh Anta. In fact, during the time of their youth it was Cheikh M'Backe who took the lead in exposing Cheikh Anta to pan-Africanism and the possibility of defeating French colonialism.

It was under the tutelage of Cheikh M'Backe that Cheikh Anta learned the dangers and terrors of French domination. Of course, this was not a one way relationship, even though the older man was quite influential. Cheikh M'Backe was impressed by the brilliance, eagerness to learn, and discipline of the young Cheikh Anta who asked him many questions and demonstrated very early the type of inquisitiveness that was necessary for superior scholarship. Always respectful of the elders the young Diop often sat with the elders while they discussed religion, politics, and history. Never one to assume an arrogant role in conversation with the elders, he practiced restraint, reflection, and repartee, of course, not on the elders but mentally, thinking, planning how to answer difficult questions by listening to the discourses of these elders of the family. He made a habit of trying to find the best metaphors, stories, traditional proverbs to make arguments. This reflection would follow him throughout his life and he would possess the same humility of character until his death.

Cheikh M'Backe believed that the capacity of the young Cheikh Anta to master the proverb wisdom of the elders and the knowledge of the imams indicated a bright destiny for the young man. He encouraged him to study diligently and to apply himself wisely. Thus, Cheikh Anta attended the French school at Diourbel but then in the 1940s went to the Lycee Faidherbe in St. Louis, at the Island of Sor, where Cheikh M'Backe was living at the time. He excelled as a student and in his chores while studying in Lycee Faidherbe.

St. Louis was the colonial capital of Senegal. It was the place where the French had established their zone of comfort. It was the center of the colonial administration but also an intellectual meeting point for Africans, the place where they came from all over the French territories and gathered to discuss the future of the colonies. From Mali, Cote D'Ivoire, Guinea, Algeria, Mauritania, Chad, Niger, Upper Volta now Burkina Faso, the intellectuals came to St. Louis because that is where the debate over the French colonial presence was most intense.

Diop's presence in St. Louis was beneficial to his intellectual growth because it allowed him to see how the French educated the Senegalese and this inspired in him a desire to resist the French colonial system. He saw the inequality, the misuse of African women by French men, particularly the creation of the large mixed population which did not exist in Dakar. He observed the divide-and-rule strategy of the French who sought to emphasize ethnic differences between the African people. Thus, before Dakar emerged as the seat of power, St. Louis, to the north of Dakar, was the cosmopolitan capital of the French African world. It had all of the contradictions of such a city and they were not lost on the young Diop.

He was literally formed in the crucible of the St. Louis of 1940–50. Among the Pan-Africanists who visited the city was one of the most powerful Black intellectuals of his day, Edward Wilmot Blyden. He found a community of young Senegalese who were devoted to revolutionary change in their condition. Blyden may have met Babacar Sy, Lamine Gueye, Ngalandou Diouf, Mar Diop, Cekuta Diop, Raoul Lonis, Lamine Senghor, Emile Faure, Adolphe Mathurin, Kojo Tuwalu, and Kouyate Garang. There is no indication that Diop met with Blyden, but the environment of St. Louis at that time makes it possible. Here was the leading Pan-Africanist in the continent, having been in Liberia, for a long time, coming to the French colonial capital to talk to the young African intellectuals of the day. It is certainly not out of the question for Diop to have met with him in the company of all the other young men of the day. The environment itself, the context maximally, the political atmosphere was hot with discussion and discourse; it was just this milieu that helped to make Cheikh Anta Diop.

It is believed that Diop was also exposed to the work of Marcus Garvey in St. Louis. A Senegalese named Sar Djim Ndiaye, who knew Cheikh Anta Diop, gave an interview a few months after the death of Cheikh Anta Diop in 1986 in which he said that he had gone to distribute Marcus Garvey information in St. Louis in the 1920s and 1930s, and his friend Sama Lam Sar recalled that the influence of Marcus Garvey was very strong in St. Louis in the period of 1930–1940. When I visited the tomb of Cheikh Anta Diop in 1990 at Caytou I was told by the elders of the village that

Cheikh had been greatly influenced by Garveyism. I have never seen this reported in any of Cheikh Anta's own writings. According to Diagne (2002:13) Diop was also influenced by the militant nationalism of Adama Lo and Lamine Gueye who became a deputy of the Palais Bourbon. Without question Diop was conversant with the works of Eric Williams, Jacques Price-Mars, Richard Wright, Louis Achille, Leopold Senghor, and R. Menil while he was at St. Louis. Of course because he was a subject of France he was also overexposed to the French philosophers, poets, scientists, and novelists. He knew French culture, it would be said, as well as any French person. Yet he would find his mission in the defense of African culture in the midst of the often, brutal quest for French domination.

There had been a tradition among the French-speaking Africans of defending the African race. In 1920 the *Messager Dahoméen* was published by Max Bloncourt and L. Hunkanrin with the idea of correcting some of the false information about the Black world. Additional books and articles were also published in this line, including *Ligue universelle de défense de la race noire* in 1924 by René Maran and Kodjo Tovalou who were influenced by Marcus Garvey. The shadow of Garvey was so huge that he cast his influence on Africans who spoke French, Portuguese, Spanish, and English. It was not unusual or abnormal to have French-speaking Africans using Garvey's arguments for advancing the race.

THE ESTABLISHMENT OF *PRÉSENCE AFRICAINE*

The journal *Présence Africaine* founded by Alioune Diop, not related to Cheikh Anta Diop, in the 1940s had a major impact on the intellectual life of Cheikh Anta Diop. It became an important outlet for his philosophical, sociological and historical work. It provided Diop and other scholars the opportunity to reach audiences of African scholars and lay persons that had never been targeted by intellectual or academic journals. Probably conceived as a more sophisticated instrument for the dissemination of Negritude writings than *Pigments*, the mimeographed student publication, *Présence Africaine* provided both an opening and an organization to the thoughts of the best African thinkers in France. Where *Pigments* was a students' paper, the new journal would be used to promote African scholarly perspectives into the French intellectual circle. Actually, Alioune Diop sought to have the French establishment bless the journal by lending their names to the editorial board. This was considered a political rather than an intellectual move by those Black intellectuals who believed that it was unnecessary for the French elite to give their names to the research interests of the African world. Cheikh Anta Diop would be the most dominant writer for the journal, thereby helping it position itself as the leading intellectual journal among Africans of any language.

Cheikh Anta Diop's importance resides in his pivotal position as the African intellectual who confronted the most powerful myth the Europeans had created about African people and our history. In 1948 he had written an explosive article for *Présence Africaine*, "When Shall We Be Able to Talk of an African Renaissance?" It would take African leaders nearly half a century to understand thoroughly the importance and complexity of this question and to create a response to it. Of course, it is fair to say that no African nation was independent at the time except Liberia and Ethiopia, and both were struggling to maintain their independence from foreign intrusion. But already Diop had seen the implication of a new birth for the continent, a new beginning after the Europeans, a renaissance of ideas, ideals, concepts, images, symbols, inventions, and relationships. All that had been broken down since the separation of the Nile Valley cultures from the rest of Africa and all that had occurred at the hands of the oppressors had to be restored, repaired, and resurrected. Who would be the Africans who would do this job?

Who are they now? The African Union under its current manifestation has assumed the burden by launching the first historic conference of African intellectuals in Dakar in October, 2004. Why would it take so many years for the African people to respond to his challenge? It must be said that Diop did not wait around for others to do the work; he found the task was to be his, much as was in his power. Later he had embarked on the long journey to re-educate the masses with his work, *Nations négres et Culture De'l antiquité negre égyptienne aux problemes culturels de l'Afrique Noire d'aujourd'hui*, published by *Présence Africaine* in 1954. Perhaps from this time forward he knew that he had placed himself in the long train of African intellectuals who sought neither glory nor wealth but the conscious and historic acknowledgement of the achievements of Black people.

SORBONNE: THE CITADEL OF THE FRENCH ACADEMY

8

In French society la Sorbonne is the Harvard, the Cambridge, the University of Sankore. It represents the highest form of scholarship, excellence in analysis and quality of inquiry that one could find in French society. To attend la Sorbonne is considered a privilege unequalled in the French academy and to write a dissertation for the university is the height of academic achievement. The young Cheikh Anta Diop entered the university with one purpose: to master the elements of Western science. However, he completed his work at la Sorbonne in an entirely new field of inquiry.

Cheikh Anta Diop wrote a doctoral thesis at the Sorbonne on the Blackness of the ancient Egyptians. This was met with hostility, derision, and rejection by the Western scholars at the Sorbonne. It was with the assistance of Louis Bachelard, the Curies, Joliot and his wife Marie, the Nobel Prize winner, who mobilized the academics in support of Diop's work that he was finally able to defend. Why was Cheikh Anta Diop's new humanism seen as a danger and fought against so vigorously by the enemies of Africa? What caused Africans themselves, often miseducated by Europe, to attack Diop? I ask these questions because when the First Congress of Black Writers and Artists was held in Paris in 1956 the African scholars understood the need to challenge the psychological hold that Europe held on their minds. By 1959 when the Second Congress was held in Rome the idea of a Greco-Latin rationalism was still a part of the discourse because there were still Africans who believed that the Greeks were the mothers and fathers of human civilization. So thorough had the indoctrination of Europe been in the academies, but more importantly, in the minds of Africans that it was easy to find Africans who would defend to the death the superiority of European culture over African culture. They had been so brainwashed by their educational experience, having read nothing of classical Africa, having denied their own intellectual existence before the arrival of Europe, and having been under the tutelage of Western philosophers and writers for so long that they were impish in their imitation of those they thought to be the mothers and fathers of human civilization. It was a scene so often repeated, that is, where the real mothers and fathers gave way to the children to be their teachers, believing that they had no existence before their children. It was into this type of intellectual chaos that Diop came as a master teacher to remove the veil from our eyes.

A SYMBIOTIC FRIENDSHIP

Cheikh Anta Diop was encouraged by the ingenuity of Alioune Diop, the thinker, philosopher, and publisher, who took courage and published the young Cheikh Anta's most famous book which was translated into English as *The African Origin of Civilization*. Educated as a scientist, Cheikh Anta Diop was interested in mastering the training to be an archaeologist, sociologist, paleontologist, economist, physicist, historian, and ethnologist. His ability to understand

African history from the earliest Nile Valley civilizations to the contemporary political moment gave him a larger view than most scholars. Diop was able to discover the key to Pharaonic society and see it as the foundation for Greek learning, thus marking a break with the long held opinion that the Greeks were the originators of civilization. At the time of Diop's contest with the Western world, the overwhelming summation of the Western writers on Africa was that it was a continent of barbarity, ignorance, lacking in originality and majesty; and on the other hand, Europe as depicted as the origin and culmination of human excellence. It is this inflated notion of Western triumphalism that Diop's work was to burst.

There is nothing so cataclysmic as the fall of an idea perched in the human mind as natural. It was the arrogance of the Western idea, the notion of European superiority that was shattered by the research of Cheikh Anta Diop. Even now, more than fifty years after Diop's first outlines of his arguments, we still have the reverberations of this incredible earthquake in European academic circles. Denials are occasionally heard as we shall see later in this volume but for the most part the scholarship of Diop and that of his colleagues and comrades profoundly alter the terms and focus of the debate among serious scholars years ago.

RESEARCH, POLITICS AND NEGRITUDE

Cheikh Anta Diop followed the classic pattern of African intellectuals by combining research interests with political actions. This combination is easily born out of an intellectual temperament which seeks to respond to the concrete conditions of people. Thus, it was Diop's belief, as it had been the belief of Dubois, Blyden, and other major African intellectuals, that it was impossible to be fully engaged in the contemporary world without utilizing one's mental gifts to work toward the liberation of the African people. It had occurred to

Diop very early that the condition of African people would not change unless one put into practice the political ideas. Without a commitment to action one could never expect to humanize the world. In this regard he was like the Negritudinist students of Paris, Aime Cesaire, Leopold Senghor, Jacques Rabemanajara, and Leon Damas. It must be remembered that when Diop defended his dissertation at the Sorbonne the first time it was Aime Cesaire who organized a celebration in his honor. Students drove through the streets of Paris blowing the horns of cars and marched with placards announcing their support for the achievement of Cheikh Anta Diop. Thus, they took action to celebrate the "victory" of Diop over the White racist professors who denied him a passing verdict. Cesaire was adamant that it was successful because of the very fact that the French professors were dumbfounded, disturbed, and angered that a Black student had the audacity to write that the ancient Egyptians were Black. So the political action of the revolutionary students, including Diop himself, would become a mantle that Diop would not be able to abandon when he returned to Dakar.

It is easy to see how Diop related to the Negritude cadre because in some ways this group was pro-African and profoundly anti-European domination. They sought to express themselves as Africans but they had no scientific base from which to do so in a thorough manner. They were, for the most part, literary men and women who were convinced that they had to show African personality through art and culture in order to be taken seriously as civilized beings. Lacking in social science or natural science skills and backgrounds, the Negritudinists were awaiting a champion who could provide authentic data to back up many of their intuitive claims.

Aime Cesaire, Leon Damas, and Leopold Senghor advanced the idea that the African personality was unique to Africans. There would be others such as Jacques Rabemanajara and a little later, Eduard Maunick, who would take up the same cause. In contemporary terms what they argued would be called an essentialist idea, but in the 1940s and 1950s the French educated Africans of the continent and the diaspora believed that their experiences in Paris had shown them that there was a real difference between European and African culture and this could only be explained in terms of the differences in personality.

The African personality was not the same as the White personality because each cultural personality had been developed in the context of its own milieu. Indeed, Leopold Senghor vehemently maintained that the African personality and quality to life was different from Western materialism. To give substance to Aime Cesaire's idea of Negritude and African Personality, the young Senghor coined the word, *Africanity*. While today the word carries with it the meaning, customs, traditions and behaviors normally associated with African experiences, among the Negritudinists it related to the entire African continent's cultural heritage (Fanon, 1967).

It was left to Cheikh Anta Diop to infuse the idea of *Africanity* with a scientific and research orientation. As a trained scientist, as well as being a student of the social sciences, Diop provided what the artists, writers, and poets could not provide for the Negritude Movement. What he knew was that the domination of European thinking over Africans had led to a displaced sense of loyalty, a disorientation of African intellectuals, and the inability of Africans to dream of overcoming the academic and intellectual deficit that had been imposed by European writers. It was not a matter of brain power, but an issue of acceptance of Europe's version of history. It is in this connection that Diop proposes the African Renaissance in 1948.

THE INFLUENCE ON STUDENTS AND YOUNG RADICALS

Most of Cheikh Anta Diop's adult life was spent without the give-and-take of university classrooms. He was alienated from the political process and from the academic process because he was an opponent of Leopold Senghor's. Diop lived in a Senegal dominated by the poet-politician Senghor and therefore had limited access to students from the university. They had to seek him out, and when they did he did not disappoint them.

Although Diop had always been involved in politics of one sort or another it was when he met a radical group of Dakar students in the 1970s that he demonstrated superior leadership and philosophical clarity in terms of his political objectives. The youth club, called Pencum Deggoo, was one of the political instruments that the young radical students used to advance a socialist and communist agenda in Senegal. It was the young people of this organization that were fundamentally influenced by Cheikh Anta Diop before he was considered a major political intellectual in the Senegalese society. This was the era of Abdoulaye Wade, who was one of the radicals and who would later become president of Senegal, himself.

In Dakar, Diop was known essentially as a political figure in the 1960s and 1970s. This did not prevent him from writing outstanding scholarship while he was engaged in trying to make life better for the Senegalese people. The 1966 Dakar Festival would make him famous among African people of the world, as one of the greatest scholars of the African world, but he would still be seen as an opposition politician in Senegal.

Diop was a true nationalist. As Dame Babou, one of Diop's political associates once said, "Cheikh Anta would say that no nation ever developed using the language of another people. Indeed, the nation that used the language of another people ran the risk of losing its own language and culture. Assimilation was death as surely as domination was death" (Babou, 2004). To say that Diop was a nationalist as a political figure is to understand him as one of the key intellectual interpreters of what it meant for Senegalese to be for themselves. When the young left wing thinkers of the Pencum Deggoo held Engels up to Diop as an example of progressive thought,

Diop's response was to ask them if they actually believed what Engels wrote when he said that Europeans were smarter than other people because they ate meat and drank milk? This question caused the young communists to reflect on the possibility that there could be an Afrocentric way of defining progress. In fact, Majmoud Diop, no relation to Cheikh Anta Diop, was the father of Senegalese communism, and one of the godfathers of the Pencum Deggo. However, it was Babacar Niang, the leader of the Parti Africaine Independence, who had brought the Pencum Deggo into interaction with Diop.

By 1977 when Dame Babou and his associates were brought into contact with Cheikh Anta Diop, the scholar had already formed his political party, Rassemblement National Democratique. Babou worked as an editor of the political newspaper because of his skill as a translator. Other young activist engaged in political dialogue and action on behalf of the party. It took strong socialist positions but it was always nationalist in outlook. These positions had been debated between Cheikh Anta Diop and his youthful followers. Thus, when Dame Babou, a central player in the editing of the paper, came to engage Diop he was soon convinced that it was possible to argue the way Cheikh argued about the future of Senegal. Most of the students accepted the fact that Senegal could never advance unless the Senegalese were in charge of their own lives. Therefore, it became simple for the Party newspaper to publish articles that would have an impact on the masses, not just the intellectuals.

The paper was published in Wolof with Arabic script, the first time that a political paper in Senegal had appealed to the masses of Senegalese in their most popular national language. Often Diop, a workaholic, completed his work in French and Dame Babou translated his articles into Wolof. They would both check the translations and then send the articles to press. Cheikh Anta Diop was a careful reader and a person who spent considerable time editing and re-editing his writings.

Always insisting that his colleagues in the Party "remove the top layers" in their analyses to discover what was under the surface of political realities, Diop became like a father to many of his younger comrades. It was his ordinariness, his humanity that endeared him to his friends and adversaries. As a political figure he did have those who held public arguments and debates with him, but he had only one major enemy, Leopold Sedar Senghor, president of the Republic of Senegal.

The great irony in the relationship between Senghor and Diop is that both of them had been educated in Paris, had been published in *Présence Africaine*, and had married French women. Diop had married Louise-Marie Maes while in Paris. He was to have four sons with her. Yet when Senghor and Diop arrived in Senegal, their paths, different in several ways, became even more radically divergent. Senghor was a Christian from the Serere ethnic group, a minority community in Senegal; Diop was a Muslim from the dominant Wolof ethnic group. But it was not so much their religion that separated them as it was their outlook on the social and economic prospects for the society. In Senegal, Senghor became the first president of the independent country of Senegal. Diop became a critical political voice in objection to the continuing dominance of France in the political and intellectual life of the country. Alongside other critics of the Senghor government, Diop articulated a Pan-African, and what must be called, Afrocentric, socialist philosophy that ran counter to Senghor's brand of French assimilationism. Senghor banned Diop from teaching at the university and made him a persona non grata in academic circles in Senegal.

I cannot say with certainty that Diop's entry into the political field as an opposition leader was due to the way he was treated by Senghor. Yet Diop continued to take an avowedly more nationalist tone. He argued that children should be taught that Egypt was a part of Africa because without knowledge of Egypt, Africans would not ever know themselves. This was a strong indication that Diop was committed to seeing Egypt as the core civilization of African antiquity even while he was developing and maintaining his political organization.

Although he usually arrived at work around 11 A.M. and left for his sister's house around 10 P.M. to eat dinner, Diop never complained of work. His chauffeur, a cousin, drove him all over town in his little Renault 4, the only car Diop ever owned. He lived meagerly without ostentation but with purpose. One does not know what type of political leader he would have been, if his party had attained the leadership of the country. Diop was not austere, but neither was he flashy. One could best describe him as a straight-arrow whose love for his family and his country was greater than his love for wealth or fame. He was interested in sports, particularly soccer, often called football by Africans, and basketball. Diop's personality was neither flamboyant nor withdrawing; it was purposeful, like a man on a mission. He enjoyed the humor that comes from witticisms, sharp words, and personal jokes. There was in him an openness to learn everything he could from anyone he could. He never saw a person of knowledge from whom he felt he could not learn from. This was most obvious in the fact that he found it easy to accord recognition to other African scholars. He mentions Theophile Obenga and Ivan Van Sertima, younger men, favorably in several of his works, encouraging their work. This was a part of Diop's attitude toward other researchers; he wanted an entire army of skilled Black scholars ready to be put at the disposal of Africa. It was this enthusiasm for African advancement that is seen in his writings.

Several scholars have written new books in French on the life of Cheikh Anta Diop. Among the more popular works are Cheikh M'backe Diop's *Cheikh Anta Diop: l'homme et l'oeuvre,* Doue Gnonsea's *Cheikh Anta Diop, Theophile Obenga: combat pour la re-naissance africaine* (2003), Pathe Diagne's *Cheikh Anta Diop et l'afrique dans*

l'histoire du monden (2002), *and* Jean Marc Ela's *Cheikh Anta Diop ou l'honneur de penser* (2000).

What is remarkable about the work of Cheikh M'backe Diop is the degree to which one of Cheikh Anta Diop's own sons has understood the work of his father. I found the book extraordinary for its completeness regarding the life of Diop. Cheikh M'backe organized the work to deal with the European domination of Africa, the African resistance, which was constant and persistent, as we had been told by Abdoulaye Wade in his book, *A Destiny for Africa*, and the various periods of Cheikh Anta Diop's life in Europe and Senegal. Many African scholars were influenced by Diop's compelling life insofar as his life was committed to the overthrow of the falsification of African history. Thus, Cheikh M'backe Diop spends considerable time examining his father's attempt to build a new African humanism.

The Western scholars, particularly the French, sought every opportunity to deny Cheikh Anta Diop a voice. They were indignant that he had the audacity to challenge their intellectual sacred cows that had been set up to maintain the notion of Western superiority. Here was a Black man who refused to imitate the pattern of research and the attitude toward Africa that had been formulated in the best schools of France.

In fact, his classic work, *Nations négres et cuture*, was phenomenal because of its challenge to the established order of Western scholarship. The text was provocative for any scholar who had argued that ancient Egypt was a White civilization. Diop shattered that perception with his powerful historical and scientific analysis.

There was an optimistic tone to his statements, sometimes pronounced as rhetorical flourishes, but always in keeping with the highest traditions of African scholarship, going back to the days of Ahmed Baba of the Sankore University of Mali. Nevertheless, he never allowed his own tradition, as a cheikh, to impose itself on him with a rigidity that would interfere with his approach to the world. He was an intellectual par excellence in the sense that he felt a commitment to all humanity. He once said:

> *"Il est indispensable de créer une équipe de chercheurs africains ou toutes les disciplines seront representées. C'est de la sorte qu'ou mettre le plus efficacement possible la pensée scientifique au service de l'Afrique.* It is essential to create a cadre of African researchers in all representative disciplines. This is what it will take to put the most efficient scientific thought to the service of Africa."

In one sense the various communities of African scholars that have been formed all over the world are a result of Diop's vision. Of course, some members of the groups have little consciousness of the fact that the organizers of the groups were influenced by Diop's call for such a community of committed African intellectuals devoted to the service of the African continent. In fact, Theophile Obenga and Cheikh M'Backe Diop started such a group in Paris. It dedicates itself to teaching the ancient classical language of Africa, *Mdw Ntr* (ancient Egyptian), to any student of the African world. The members are professional people from physics, engineering, computer technology, and information sciences. This is as it should be because they are demonstrating that it is possible to create such a group and build a foundation for future work. The Afrocentric Circle at Temple University led by Ama Mazama, particularly as it is expressed in the Nommo meetings, is such a gathering. In Philadelphia we have established the Free African University with monthly meetings on topics of interest to the African world. At a grander scale, the African Union under the influence of President Abdoulaye Wade, President Thabo Mbeki, and President Joachim Chissano, sought to energize a congress of African intellectuals from around the world to assist the continent. This is the practical vision of Cheikh Anta

Diop's call for a cadre of researchers who would put "la pensée scientifique au service de l'Afrique."

CONTINENTAL AFRICAN AND DIASPORAN SCHOLARS

For Diop it was essential that African scholars from various societies be involved in the process of resurrecting the continent. It did not matter to him that the Africans were from the United States, Brazil, Jamaica, or Gabon, or any other place where Black people lived. What was important for Diop's vision was that the African intellectual be committed to bringing about a revolution in the way Africa is conceived and developed. The Black researcher must have at least a full commitment. He believed that scholars from history, linguistics, sociology, geology, and all other fields should be dedicated to this project to raise the standards of interrogation of African sources. One does not have to allow the historians to do this work as if there is nothing that you can do. We all have a responsibility as intellectuals to resist the degradation of Africa. In every area where the African scholar has capacity, there will be issues that must be confronted.

Nothing distinguishes Diop from his contemporaries on the African continent more than his belief in a Pan-African response to the historical problems of the Black World. This is an achievement that is rarely discussed yet it is at the heart of his desire to see a cadre of scholars committed to the general process of developing an African consciousness. While he had not traveled in the diaspora as he would have desired, he found it important to read the younger scholars such as Ivan Van Sertima and Walter Rodney of Guyana as well a the older scholars such as John Henrik Clarke and Carter G. Woodson of the United States. He was familiar with the leading essayists and novelists of the diaspora but he remained essentially alone in his passion for a collective sense of Africa's history. I am certain that his pan-

Africanism was fueled by what he had seen in Paris with the large numbers of Africans arriving from the colonies with little or no understanding of our general condition. This was so whether those Blacks arriving in Paris came from Africa or the Caribbean.

Being a humanist of the highest order Cheikh Anta Diop believed that the destruction of the environment, the lack of literacy, famine, ethnic tensions, disease, and resource exploitation were all issues that could be dealt with effectively by encouraging intellectuals to devote their time and energy to the re-invigoration of African ideals. Given Diop's concern with the re-energizing of Africa it is easy to assume that he was an idealist with no concreteness but this would be a long way from the truth. Diop was a practical man and he took seriously his attempt to discover in the people the longing for a correction of history. He wrote to this longing. His science was meant for something in the strictest African way; it was not science for the sake of science.

Ultimately, however, Diop was fundamentally committed to the idea of the cultural unity of Africa and all intellectuals, if they were truly African intellectuals, had to work toward an African solution of the problems of ethnic tensions and distrust. This could be done by understanding the "*personnalitè culturelle africaine*" (Diop, 1991, 227). Naturally some of Diop's ideas had been stirred by the Negritudinists in Paris. They had raised questions of culture and of personality in such a way as to suggest almost mystical qualities of human beings. Diop would have none of this. He would not engage in a theological or mystical discussion with anyone about the African personality. What he saw were the concrete conditions of the African people and he knew that those conditions had been created by slavery, exploitation, and colonialism. He did not seek accommodation, but a way to overturn the results of that oppression. This means that he relied upon science to define new realities instead of producing rhetoric without work.

We could never be free, and remain free, unless we located ourselves in the realm of African consciousness. But consciousness grows out of information and knowledge and this is a historical process. Diop knew that the cultural unity of Africa had to be established in order to keep Africans from taking anti-African positions. If people could see that they have similar histories and origins, then they would more easily see the unity in their cultures.

Thus, it was Diop's work to demonstrate a methodology for studying the unity of Africa. Two approaches emerged from his work. First, he examined a set of themes that were essential to an understanding of African cultures in a comparative sense. In this regard, Cheikh Anta Diop was among the first African scholars to propose a comparative approach to the study of Africa. Secondly, he always emphasized the anteriority of ancient Kemet in his discussions of the connectedness of African cultures.

DIOP IN THE AMERICAN CONTEXT

Much like Aime Cesaire of the Negritude school and the great Afro-Cuban poet, Nicolas Guillen, Diop had no particular desire to visit America. He found the country distant from his own political orientations. Like Cesaire and Guillen he had seen the discrimination measured out to Black people in the United States and wanted no part of the racist situations America had come to be known for throughout Europe and Africa. While we may argue that Europeans were just as racists, we cannot deny the fact that there was an especially virulent form of racist violence in America that would have caused any clear-thinking African to have second thoughts about visiting such a country. Diop had such feelings.

Although Diop found America's intellectual world strange; he had wanted only to please his African American audience and so he came, he saw, and he enjoyed the manner in which he was lionized by the Africans in America. His tour of Atlanta and Washington brought him in close contact with an audience that had waited for his coming since the English translation of *Nations negres et culture* and *The African Origin of Civilization*.

It was the efforts of a strong group of scholars and pan-Africanists centered in Atlanta that made it possible for Cheikh Anta Diop to visit the United States. A number of individuals were associated with Diop's visit, including Asa Hilliard, Larry Williams, Charles Finch, Listervelt Middleton, Leonard Jeffries, and others. On the occasion of his lecture tour, Diop was interviewed by the outstanding media personality, Listervelt Middleton, whose career had seemed primed particularly for this historic moment.

Although the interview with Listervelt Middleton became one of the most retaped and recirculated intellectual works in the history of the African American community, Diop's main purpose in coming to the United States, which he had avoided as long as possible, was to be the key personality and scholar at the "Man and His Civilizations" conference convened at Morehouse College at the Martin Luther King, Jr. International Chapel in April, 1985. Among the honors received by Diop from the African American community was an honorary doctorate from Morehouse College, one of the nation's best predominantly African colleges, and the keys to the city of Atlanta by Mayor Andrew Young who declared April 4, 1986 "Cheikh Anta Diop Day" in Atlanta.

AN AFRICAN HERO

Diop remains an African hero to his African American audiences by virtue of his anti-racist and anti-classist positions. But beyond his politics, he is seen, among all African intellectuals, as the one who has exhibited the greatest courage in confronting head-on the maligning of African civilization and history. He fought the enemies of Africa, not on superstition or good-feelings, but on science and detailed scholarship. His gift to other scholars was never to accept the inferiorizing of African people. Any theory and any analysis that seems to suggest that African people are less than any other people in any field must be looked at with severe criticism. One can never accept the arguments of the enemies of Africa about Africa. For Diop, nothing ate at the heart of the African world more than the European constructed notions of dominance based on the idea that the evolution of science led directly to their civilization. Thus, he shows that the highest civilization in antiquity was a Black civilization and that any structure Europe used to build upon must have been laid by those who came first according to science. Diop does not gloat over this or any other fact; it is simply the way history must be seen. Blacks have no special gifts because our history is the first recorded human history. It should be clear that Diop is not making a racist argument in his works; he is making an anti-racist argument.

Cheikh Anta Diop is in a class alone by virtue of his struggles and victories in forcing the academy to pay attention to the work of African scholars who were not supported by the universities but who nevertheless had prepared themselves as well as any of those who taught in the universities to delve into research. In this sense, Diop was a model for activist, committed scholarship.

I think Diop believed that Europe had insinuated itself into every corner of African history as an enemy of the African people. It was not a recent insertion, but an old one, organized and gathered during the earliest years of Western science. As Europeans, or those who would now be called Europeans, developed their sciences, they saw in African art, culture, and science much to be emulated. What they did, of course, was to falsify, deny, malign, and barbarize the historical records. But that is not all that they did. Diop understood before most major African scholars that it was Europe's idea to distort the psychology of humanity in order to advance White supremacy. Thus, Diop writes that Galen, the Greek physician, who lived in the second century A.D. reduced the characteristics of the Black man to two traits: an inordinately long penis, and a strong propensity for laughter (Diop, 1981:216). It was clear to Diop that for Galen, "these two traits, one physical and one moral, were enough to characterize the generic type of Black. Even though Galen regularly visited the library of the temple at Memphis, where he was the last Greek scholar, six centuries after Hippocrates, to consult Imhotep's annals, the brilliance of Egyptian civilization was about to be forgotten and Rome was dominating the world."

Clearly Diop is disturbed by the fact that the Greeks not only used the information that they obtained from the annals of Imhotep and made African knowledge their own but attempted to dehumanize the people from whom they got the knowledge. Indeed, Diop argued that the most famous Greek ideas, those of Plato and Aristotle, had originated in Africa. Furthermore, "if certain of Plato's ideas have become obscure, it is because we fail to place them in the context of their Egyptian source" (Diop, 1974:232). Thus, it is not simply a matter of the enslavement of Africans that brought about the Western conception of Africans as inferior because of physical differences, it was something that was found in the West's earlier response to the magnificence of Africa. It is probably something as simple as cultural envy that gave birth to the lies about Africa.

At any rate, Diop knew that the cultural opinions and caricatured identifications beginning with some psychological traits wrongly construed were the basis for the ideological work of Count Arthur Gobineau and other racists. They defined Europeans from a standpoint of Apollonian rationality, a superior quality, and Africans from the standpoint of emotional sensibility.

Gobineau's nonsense was palpable. It emerged out of the consciousness of Europeans in much the same way as it had been formulated earlier in the caricatures of Galen. In fact, Gobineau had written that the quality most missing in African people was thought itself (Gobineau, *Essai sur l'égalite des races humaines*, Book II, Chapter VII). If thought is missing, reason is missing, and without reason, one cannot talk about Black people creating civilizations. Gobineau writes that "among all the art forms that the dark-skinned creature prefers, music holds first place, because it caresses his ear with a succession of sounds and requires nothing of the thinking part of the brain. . . . How foreign he remains to the delicate conventions for which the European imagination has learned to ennoble its senses. . . . The White's illuminated sensuality, directed by science and thought, with the first notes, as they say, begins to create a picture. . . ." (Gobineau, Book II, Chapter VII). Gobineau does not finish with this flourish against Africans; he continues in this section with an explanation that the Bamana people of Mali reacts in an emotional way to music but does not have the intellectual faculty to respond to it in a proper intelligent, reasonable way. Of course, this is nonsense and Diop's response is pithy. "The Egyptian civilization, with its grandiose art, entirely due to a Black people, is the most categorical refutation of Gobineau's 'scholarly' inanity, and we will not even bother to criticize his constellation of errors" (Diop, 1981:217).

Gobineau and others created an atmosphere in the West that was anti-African and anti-Black and generated the greatest amount of race conscious writing the world had ever seen. The Western scholars of the 19th and 20th centuries, who looked at Africa, saw only through the lens that had been given to them by earlier racist writers. And while Africans themselves were often unaware of the gathering storm of bias attacks against African civilization the Europeans were mustering their propaganda weapons.

Diop's lament is that the Negritude poets could not defend Africa and Africans from these psychological, pseudo-scientific, and anti-historical assaults because as poets they had no way to see the errors of science. They did not have the ability to refute these errors and in fact some of them gave the impression that our culture, as negatively defined by the Whites, was in fact something of value. They took on the idea of a submissive culture and sought to use it to assert value. Therefore, as Diop (1981:218) pointed out, the Negritude writers "accepted this so-called inferiority and boldly assumed it in full view of the world. Aime Cesaire shouted: 'Those who explored neither the seas nor the sky', and Leopold S. Senghor: 'Emotion is Negro and Reason is Greek'."

The African participation in the process of inferiority, that is, the acceptance of White definitions of Africans, is at the root of the problem in the early twentieth century. Diop is aware of the problem. Since everyone was led by the Western writers down the slippery slope of White racial superiority and Black racial inferiority as defined by the issues of reason and emotion it was difficult to get even Black writers to see that this personality, psychological factor, as Diop (Ibid.) calls it, was nothing but what is called national temperament. Diop explains that it "varies from the Slav to the German, from the Latin to the Papua." One could, in that case, speak of the English temperament, the French temperament, the Kenyan temperament, the Chinese temperament, and so forth. However, when the Negritude writers affirmed the negative ideas of Blacks that had been spewed forth by racist writers they embraced an attitude of acceptance that would eat away at every Black thinker, writer, artist, and conscious individual who knew that it was not so, but who was told over and over again that it was so, and it would become an intellectual disaster. How to prevent this continuing degradation of African people became the biggest project in Diop's life. What must one do to overcome years of insulting researches and essays and reports by institutes? In the first place, one must challenge the science itself by aggressively fighting to demonstrate that poor science is the basis of all racist constructions and that Whites have been on a centuries-old campaign against African people.

Understanding the challenge it was Diop's idea to make a difference in the world by contesting the most prominent issues raised in history and linguistics. This would be the battleground, but he also had the clarity to see that he had to work on the psychological issue as well because it was not only Blacks who had suffered from racist science but also Whites had been fooled into accepting these falsifications themselves. They built their lives and careers on bad science, and also they had to be corrected as well. What Galen had unleashed in the second century A.D. was finally being challenged by the twentieth century pharaoh of African history.

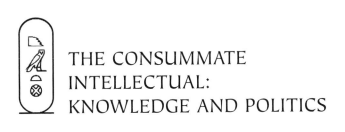

CHAPTER 2

THE CONSUMMATE INTELLECTUAL: KNOWLEDGE AND POLITICS

AN AUTHENTIC INTELLECTUAL

Cheikh Anta Diop was not an intellectual because the European world said he was an intellectual; in fact, he was never accorded any real recognition among White scholars. However, it is true that near the end of his life, the University of Lille in France asked him to serve on a doctoral dissertation committee. This request, which Diop did not accept, was made by Professor Vercoutter whom Diop had confronted at the 1974 UNESCO conference in Cairo. Diop received neither the Croix de Guerre, the Medal of Honor, the Pulitzer, nor the Nobel Prize. He sat in no endowed chair at any major Western institution and was barred for most of his career from teaching at the National University in Senegal. Yet he remains the most penetrating figure in our African intellectual tradition because he went directly to the core of racist reasoning and defeated it in its lair. There was no vulgar search for career in his life; there was only duty to truth. Indeed, soon after his death the University of Dakar was renamed Université de Cheikh Anta Diop (UCAD).

It is true that some Whites grudgingly respected the work he did and cited him, often erroneously, in an effort to build their own careers by trying to bash Black scholarship. Of course, it has not always been White scholars who have challenged the work of Diop; many Black authors have taken their shots at him as well. In any case, few of them have read Diop enough to present a strong argument against his work. It would have been possible for Diop and his research to have been disastrous for the Black world, if he had made claims that were easily refuted. In that case his work would have been indefensible and the enemies of Africa and the Afrocentric idea would have found him easy prey. As it turns out they cannot refute his research and have had to resort to name-calling such as is done by the apologist Clarence Williams in his book, *L'Impossible Retour* (2004). Williams, one of the most ardent critics of Afrocentric writers, is guilty of the worst type of dispersion casting against all Afrocentric scholarship. Such a writer finds Diop's positions contradictory to their Eurocentric training and consequently they are not able to process what they read. If Diop claims that the ancient Egyptians were Black; these writers claim that Diop must be out of his mind. If Diop claims that Africans emerged from a matriarchal cradle, then you will have the naysayers saying, without proof, that it is not so.

Diop was an intellectual because he understood that the premises of research and scholarship were openness to all forms of knowledge, comprehensive reading and study, and critical analysis. He did not let Western scholarship dictate to him; he studied it, mastered it, and then demonstrated its racist bias. But in order to perform as he did meant that he had to interrogate the research of Western scholars. One cannot take a petty attitude toward the reflection of others without being called petty oneself. This is what Diop avoided by a close reading and location of all the Western writers he criticized. To advance African research he had to take seriously the anthropology, history, and linguistics that had been produced by Europeans. What aided Diop and what has assisted most of the critical work done by African scholars is the fact that during the period of European triumphalism most of the writers of Europe wrote self consciously as Europeans. They were dominant in the production of literary and historical works during a time when Africa's voice was barely heard above the shouts of the colonial officers.

THE PASSION FOR LEARNING

Diop believed that the scholar had to be consumed with a passion for learning. He did not believe that one had to accept everything that one had read but it was essential to read everything or as nearly as possible all that one could read on a particular subject. Recognizing that every language had its own special characteristics and ways of delivering information, Diop applied himself to the study of languages. Thus, the value of Diop's study, particularly in terms of the study of African languages, is that he was able to tease out meanings and connections that escaped the ordinary person reading from French or English. Knowing the ancient Egyptian language helped him to see the relatedness to other African languages. If you do not know Peul, Wolof, or Akan, it is not possible for you to even speculate on the connections and correspondences found between those languages and ancient Egyptian. Thus, the mastery of languages was one of the key elements in Diop's quest as an intellectual.

In 1974 UNESCO organized a conference to be held in Cairo from January 28-February 3 on the "Peopling of Egypt and the Decipherment of the Meroitic Script." Among the persons invited to participate in the conference were some of the greatest names in European scholarship on ancient Africa. In addition to the African giants, Cheikh Anta Diop and Theophile Obenga, the other major players at the conference were W. Kaiser, Germany; J. Leclant, France; R. El Nadoury, Egypt; S. Sauneron, France; T. Save Soderbergh, Sweden; and P. L. Shinnie, Canada (Diop, 2003:297). All had reputations in their countries for the work they had done on ancient Egypt. Shinnie was one of the leaders in the field of Nubian studies. El Nadoury, technically from Africa, leaned more toward the Western interpretation, although he could not resist the overwhelming documentation of Cheikh Anta Diop and Theophile Obenga.

The papers at Cairo established Diop and his protégée, Theophile Obenga, as two of the most important African scholars in the world. This conference was to establish Diop's international credentials and place him in the middle of the discourse on the peopling of Egypt. It created for Theophile Obenga, a young scholar, an intense mission to carry out the project that had been started in Cairo. But the UNESCO conference in Cairo would unite many of the European scholars against the work of Diop. Indeed, Jean Leclant and J. Vercoutter took a personal interest in debating many of the ideas advanced by Diop at the conference. Among the many demonstrations undertaken by Diop at Cairo was the grammatical relationship between ancient Egyptian, Wolof, and Coptic.

One could see that the UNESCO conference, although under the direction of Maurice Glele, as UNESCO's representative, was designed to reinforce the generally accepted idea at the time that ancient Egypt was a White civilization. The Western scholars who had been called to the conference in Cairo came from the most prestigious institutions in Europe and Canada, only two Southern Africans were invited to the conference, Diop and Obenga. When the conference was over it was clear that no one could ever again discount the interconnections between ancient Egypt and the rest of Africa. It was clear that African civilization was older than that of Europe, but also the classical civilizations of Africa were Black civilizations.

LINGUISTIC CORRESPONDENCES
AND OTHER LANGUAGE STUDIES

In Senegal, scholars such as Pathe Diagne, Aboubacry Moussa Lam and others have risen to take on the work started by Diop. Diagne has made some interesting discoveries, including correspondences between African ethnic groups and American Indians. On the other hand, Lam has sought to demonstrate how the people of West Africa were migrants from the East as seen in the languages of Western Africa. The languages are directly related to languages of the Nile Valley. According to Lam, the migration of the people often called Peul, Pular, Fulbe, or Fulani, can be traced across the Sahel from the East by examining place names of towns and villages. This will be discussed further when we consider Diop's evidence.

What distinguished Diop's mode of linguistic thinking from that of other African authors at the time? I believe it was the exceptional sense of the interconnections that had to exist between African languages. Diop was unconvinced by the European authors that Africans, on the same continent, could be looked at as having no connections with each other. He did not believe it; indeed, it was an insult to his understanding and his experiences as an African. Diop refused to accept the idea that African history began when the Europeans became aware of it. There have always been Africans who understood that their mission was to bring about a transformation in the way African history and culture was taught.

Alain Anselin, the leading Caribbean Egyptologist, has argued that Diop utilized linguistic similarities to make his points (Anselin, 2000:79). Anselin is correct to see Diop's concentration on the linguistic data as important, but this was not his only course of action. Diop was eager to demonstrate through careful research and investigation in history that all cultures of Africa could be connected through concrete reference to historical phenomena. One did not have to imagine that the Akan had anything to do with the Sahel states, one simply had to follow the oral traditions to appreciate the connectedness that existed. This was true all over the continent as Africa was a continent on the move. People have traveled, migrated, and explored the continent longer than they have done so in any other region of the world.

HISTORY AND THE POLITICAL UNION OF AFRICA

Diop argued more than any other African intellectual of his time for the uniting of the continent. He was a visionary, seeing all the possibilities of unity, and hoping that the political leaders would have the ability to participate in that vision. Given the fact, that he practiced history, Diop believed that all knowledge had a purpose or at least was used for a purpose. His system of thinking was not fragmentary, but wholistic when it came to appreciating the role history played in the affairs of the world. It might be said that he was responding to the overwhelming influence of European assertion in the African world. I would have no quarrel with that characterization except to argue in extension that the European assertion was an abnormality of history and Diop was concerned with correcting all abnormalities. Indeed, the term "falsification of history" is used by Diop to describe this abnormal European approach to history.

CONCERNING DIOP'S CRITICS

Diop's positions have agitated an entirely new cadre of popular White writers or writers who write White. One such writer with a racist ideology is Dinesh D'Souza, an Indian author who is particularly keen on advancing a White point of view. His books have always sought to attack Black people and Black resistance to White supremacy. In fact, he argues that ". . . Afrocentrism fundamentally remains a pedagogy of initiation into a new form of Black consciousness and also into manhood." Given this Eurocentric view of Africology, D'Souza (1995:360) seeks to demonstrate that was not racist; that segregation was established by paternal Whites to protect the former slaves; and especially that "Egypt was a multiracial society" (Ibid:367) dominated by White skinned Egyptians, and that the only time that Blacks/Africans ruled Egypt, was during the

Nubian dynasty (Ibid:368). It goes without saying that this type of racist and right wing drivel has become a common part of the anti-African school of thought.

Many people have written about Diop in one way or the other, but one notes that among Western writers there has been a stream of ideological asides and rhetorical diversions about his scholarship (Diop, 1991). Although they mentioned Diop's name they do not engage his scholarship. Rather they attack his motives, ideology, and sometimes character. This shows the weakness of their arguments and the strength of Diop's argument for the African origin of civilization. Such is the case with the limited appreciation of the deep structure of Diop's analysis among scholars such as Lefkowitz (1992) and Baines (1991).

For example Lefkowitz writes an attack on Afrocentric scholars in *The New Republic* (1992), and summarizes the extensive work of Cheikh Anta Diop without ever quoting his arguments. Thus, she raises the spectre of Diop (1974) but never presents any evidence to dispute the findings of Diop. Another review of Diop was written by Baines, a compatriot of Lefkowitz, for the *New York Times Book Review* (1991). Baines (1991) simply in discussing Diop that ". . . the evidence and reasoning used to support the arguments are often unsound" without showing us where that evidence is unsound. Pronouncements are not evidence and cannot be taken seriously by scholars or lay people.

Therefore, Baines like so many Eurocentric writers are asking readers, particularly White readers, to reject the thesis that Africa was significant in the rise of world civilization because Diop's is not following the script laid down by Europeans. Diop has introduced significant evidence for the African origin of civilization as well as for the historical fact that the ancient Egyptians were black-skinned. In the same review Baines attacks Diop's work, *Civilization or*

Barbarism, for not being original; yet he does not dispute any of the facts presented in the monumental work. Perhaps the question is not is the work original but is it factual? Of course, neither Baines nor any of his colleagues are eager to answer that question. It is a typical tactic that we have seen so many times when African scholars, either on the continent or in the diaspora, present research: attack the person or reject the argument but do not engage any evidence. To refute anyone's thesis it is important to present evidence not rely on your own claim to credentials.

CHAPTER 3

EVIDENCES OF ARCHAEOLOGY, LANGUAGE AND CULTURE

THE ARCHAEOLOGY OF IDENTITY

Perhaps more than anyone else it was Diop who taught us that archaeological research would be a major source of information about Africa's past. There is an unparalleled record of early humans on the continent of Africa and this provides the researcher with useful information about the movement of humans, the domestication of animals, the harvesting of grain, and the settling of communities. It was the purpose of Diop to assist scholars in understanding the relationship of oral narratives, rock art, and the testimony of archaeology and linguistics in studying the rise of civilization. All study and research were to support what Zewde (2002:12) calls "assertion of . . . continental unity and its primacy in the history of the world as the cradle of mankind."

It is Diop's evidence of the Black origin of ancient Egypt that created most opposition to his theories. In his book, *The African Origin of Civilization*, Cheikh Anta Diop challenged the idea that the ancient Egyptians were other than Black. He wrote in the chapter "Origin of the Ancient Egyptians," that there were eleven arguments to prove the Blackness of the ancient Egyptians. Diop's arguments for the Black origin of ancient Egyptians may be categorized in four groups: (1) physical evidence, (2) human images, (3) testimony of ancient writers, and (4) sacred epithets. The physical evidence was based on anthropological measurements of predynastic skulls. Diop examined width of face, nasal length, cephalic index, and facial index in order to say that the population of Kemet was Black in pre-dynastic times. He also looked at osteological data, something known as the "Lepsius canon" which said that the typical African of this period was "the short armed negrito type." Another physical experiment had to do with blood type. The blood type of ancient Egyptians was B, the predominant type among other Black Africans. This contrasts with the European blood type that is typically A2.

The human images found on the walls of temples and tombs underscored Diop's argument that the ancient Africans of Egypt never painted themselves as Whites but always as black or brown-skinned people. He used a number of images to make this point, including the evidence from the bas reliefs, particularly the Biban-el-Moluk bas relief and the Ramses III tomb ethnology. Diop contended that the ancient Egyptians were Black because all of the classical authors who were in the position to know witnessed the skin color of the ancient Egyptians and were agreement that they were Black. He was able to cite Herodotus in the 5th century B.C., Aristotle in the 4th century B.C., Lucian in the 2nd century B.C., Strabo in the 1st century, and Diodorus of Sicily in the 1st century A.D. All of these writers and others attested to the fact that the ancient Egyptians were Black. The myth of the Whiteness of the ancient Egyptians was one of the great falsifications of history. Diop saw it as the underpinning of the Western assertion of superiority over the African and the African continent. If Europe could get away with "stealing" the past of Africa and appropriating the most majestic civilization of the ancient African world as European it would be able to control the African mind forever. It was essential that African scholars break this bondage.

But these arguments and evidences were not the only supports for the principal position of Diop. Indeed, his thesis is also bolstered by the fact that divinities, gods, deities were often shown as black. Furthermore, one can see many cultural similarities with other African cultures, particularly the concepts of circumcision and totemism. In addition to these points, Diop makes the point that the ancient Egyptian language shows many correspondences with other African languages. This linguistic relationship has been taken up by other scholars as evidence that Egypt was one of the earliest classical civilizations of Africa. Works by Diop, Mozer, Niagaran-Bouah, and Obenga, as well as Bilolo, establish the proposition that ancient Egypt must be seen as integrally connected to the emergence of African cultures elsewhere. It is Obenga's (Obenga, 1992, 1993) work that has articulated the ways ancient Egyptian and Coptic are related as well as to show the non-existence of the so-called Hamito-Semitic thesis of African languages.

Not only were the ancient Egyptians Black, they were related to other Blacks. Indeed, "In Zimbabwe—which may well be an extension of the land of the Macrobian Ethiopians mentioned by Herodotus—we find ruins of monuments and cities built of stone, with the falcon represented" (1974:157). What is so interesting about these ruins is that they are stretched over an area about the size of France. Only when writers come to know the extent of the falsification of Black history can they react in an intelligent manner. Consider the fact that the basic organization and conception of the Egyptian civilization is absolutely not White or Western; it is profoundly Black. Diop (1974:187) says, "This is confirmed by our knowledge that the basic elements of Egyptian civilization are neither in Lower Egypt, nor in Asia, nor in Europe, but in Nubia and the heart of Africa; moreover that is where we find the animals and plants represented in hieroglyphic writing."

THE ARCHAEOLOGY OF ORIGINS

Diop's principal theses were based on the archaeology of his day. This means that his evidence, as thorough as it was, only extended to the 1980s. What we know now is that all scientific data suggest that all living humans share a single African ancestor, a woman who lived about 200,000 years ago and whose descendants replaced an earlier human species. Although it has long been accepted that human evolution began in Africa nearly 6 million years ago with the appearance of hominids in Chad, the more popular information, likely present for Diop's work, was the fact that *homo habilis* appeared about 2.5 million years ago. About a million years ago there appeared *homo erectus*, the first human ancestor to migrate to southern Eurasia from Africa. Years after Diop's hypothesis, the late Allan C. Wilson, while at the University of California in Berkeley, established that the first modern humans arose in Africa about 166,000 to 249,000 years ago. A workable chronology of hominids and humans is as follows:

 40

Ardipithecus ramidus	5 million
Australopithecus anamensis	4 million
Australopithecus afarensis	4.2 million
Australopithecus Bahr el Ghazali	3.5 million
Australopithecus Africanus (Dinqnish)	3.3 million
Australopithecus boiser	2.5 million
Australopithecus Garhi	2.5 million
Australopithecus robustus	2.0 million
Homo habilis	1.9 million
Homo ergaster	1.9 million
Homo erectus	1.8 million
Homo neanderthalensis	300,000
Homo sapiens sapiens	250,000
Omo Valley	
Grimaldi	
Cro Magnon	

Congo-South Africa Cultures	180,000
Esna, Egypt	20,000
Luiza	11,500

Diop was one of the first African scholars to embrace the scientific method to prove that Africa was the origin of the human race. He also knew that there would be other discoveries or disclosures in Africa that would further establish it as the homeland of the humans. While he did not have yet the information that was to be revealed from the Awash River banks and Omo River Valley in Ethiopia, Diop had enough to believe that the records of human origins would not be contradicted. We have since learned more detail about the direct human ancestor, *Australopithecus afarensis*, dating from 3.5 to 4.2 million years ago. The initial find in 1974, just a few months before the Cairo conference, was of a female skeleton called "Dinqnesh" although many in the West knew her by the name "Lucy." Dinqnesh means "you are wonderful." Numerous other discoveries were made in the triangle of Great Rift Valley. This is an area where the Great Rift Valley forms a wide low-lying triangle.

Diop does not deal extensively with Ethiopia, yet in many ways it might be the mother of Egyptian civilization (ben-Jochannan, 1971, 1972, 1988). I can see future scholars exploring the meaning of the Stone Age and pre-Stone Age cultures who used flint stones that are now being found in the river beds all over Eastern Africa. There are delicate, sensitive cave drawings in Ethiopia that have been dated to half a million years. The research agenda for African scholars in the next generation is full. It cannot be an agenda driven by the granting agencies of the West; it must be an agenda drawn up in the research interest of Africa.

There is richness in Ethiopia that has not been adequately developed because non-Ethiopians have often been in charge of interpreting a large part of Ethiopian origins as foreign without understanding the interactions between peoples. More than forty different ethnic groups live in Ethiopia. It is not possible to speak confidently about Southern Arabians bringing culture to Ethiopia given the facts on the ground. Can we talk about interactions? Of course, we can and must appreciate the fact that at some moments in history people from Ethiopia dominated southern Arabia. Many of these Arabs were brought into Ethiopia with the returning Ethiopians. One is to understand this situation in the context of African not Arab history. What the people of Ethiopia built in Africa was never built in Asia by the Arabs. Were there linguistic influences? Perhaps there are certain languages of Africa that have Arabic influence, but this does not make them Arabic languages. It is as if English would be called Latin because nearly seventy percent of the vocabulary is Latin.

Egypt, in Africa, provides us with the longest record of written history as the continent of Africa itself provides the world with the longest evidence of human habitation. In order to investigate these two issues, Egyptian history and archaeological records, Cheikh Anta Diop used every discipline at his disposal to establish the African story. He was grounded in numerous languages and sciences, knowledgeable of physics, interested in oral narratives, a student of the material artifacts of African people, and capable of interpreting sources of information about the African past because of his general outlook on the world. He believed that the Western scholars had used false information to support the domination of colonized people. In many ways Diop was following the path of African scholars like William Leo Hansberry, Carter G. Woodson and W. E. B. Du Bois in his appreciation of archaeology. This emphasis on archaeological research is evident in the writings of DuBois (1915, 1946), and Woodson (1936, 1949). Of course, neither Hansberry, who did not write much, nor Woodson or Du Bois would make the same use of archaeology as Diop.

The African past is of preeminent importance to world history. It is on the African continent where we discover the earliest creativity and

42

maintenance of civilization by hominids. Every major developmental stage of humankind can be demonstrated from records on the African continent. Furthermore, Africa was the initial home of the cultivation of vegetable foods and dry-grown cereals. Along with these developments and the domestication of animals came the rise of the literate societies along the Nile, particularly Kemet, Nubia, and Axum. But all of the civilized societies find their origin in the fact that the earliest hominids were Africans. It is accepted that between six million and four million years ago the first creatures acknowledged as hominids appeared in Africa. Almost all of the fossils from this period illustrate the fact that Africa is the seat of the monogenesis of *homo sapiens.*

We know that the earliest representatives of the genus *Homo,* to which all modern humans belong, may date between two and four million years ago in Northeast Africa. Southern Africa has also shown evidence of early fossil remains. In *Civilization or Barbarism: An Authentic Anthropology,* Diop explores the latest research available to him and concludes that Leakey's research on the origin of *homo sapiens* in East Africa was sound argumentation for the African origin of humanity.

What is more stunning is the fact that contemporary researchers in Africa have continued to prove the points that were suggested in the writings of Cheikh Anta Diop. Indeed, British archaeologists discovered that the desert areas of Egypt have been quite rich in human settlement. Indeed in 2003 the team found 30 sites that were rich in art chiseled into rocks. These sites have been dated to 4000 B.C. We know that sites have been discovered in the Western desert and in Chad much older than these sites from the Eastern Desert, that is, the Nubian Desert. The rock drawings demonstrate that the African people had conceptions of communication long before they established the unified state of Kemet. In fact, the drawings show cattle, goats, ostriches, giraffes, hippopotamuses, boats, and the people of the area. What could have made these people draw pictures of giraffes and hippos? Were they speculating or did they live an existence where these animals were prevalent? Did they move from such an area and these pictures were simply images that they remembered in their earlier lives? In other words, were these drawings evidence of epic memory?

Diop (1974:xiv) had written in *The African Origin of Civilization* that "the history of Black Africa will remain suspended in air and cannot be written correctly until African historians dare to connect it with the history of Egypt. In particular, the study of languages, institutions, and so forth, cannot be treated properly, in a world, it will be impossible to build African humanities, a body of African human sciences, so long as that relationship does not appear legitimate." There is no puzzle to this conception, no complexity on the face of it; Diop's proposal is plausible.

EARLY AND CLASSICAL CIVILIZATIONS OF AFRICA

In *Precolonial Black Africa,* Diop is concerned with the falsifications fed by European writers about the inability of Africans to govern themselves, to create civilizations, and to maintain political and civil discipline, thus he researches and presents in this book the overwhelming evidence of African social political evolution. Turning to the issue of the caste system that was found in West Africa before the coming of the White man, Diop argues that there were three classes of citizens, the *ger*, comprising the nobles and farmers, the *neno*, with the following, goldsmiths, etc., and the *djam*, those who are unfree. For him, this constituted a caste system but it was unlike the Indian caste system. The evolution of the ancient city in Europe is discussed with an eye toward how it differed from the developments in Africa. In Europe, the idea of cities was an idea about security, about fortresses, about fortifications, about protecting property and lives. In Africa, the idea of the city was about spiritual places where men and women gathered to carry out the rituals and festivals that sustained the people. It was a different concept than what evolved in the West where the city was first a fortress such as Troy, Sparta, Athens, and Rome. The walls around the cities were meant to hold back the chaos, greed, lust, and violence of the outside world. This is not the same for the city in Africa. It was a much more open place where the people met to trade, to gossip at the wells, and to share stories of personal and collective triumph.

Diop's detractors always had something negative to say about Africa. Well, Africans do not have constitutions to govern their behaviors and therefore cannot be considered equal to European states. This type of argument Diop found ludicrous as if it was Africa's objective to be equal to Europe. His point was that one cannot make claims without understanding the cultural history of the people about whom you are making claims.

The idea of a Constitution, Diop argued, was not foreign to Africa. In fact, the Mossi Constitution is a remarkable instrument of governance as is the Cayor Constitution. Diop argues that the Mossi government in Burkina Faso, is a constitutional monarchy. Having experienced first hand the operation of the Mossi court I can attest to Diop's description of this constitutional monarchy that still exists in its traditional form under the modern state system. The way the system works is like this:

The emperor, the Moro Naba, comes by heredity from the family of the previous Moro Naba (eleventh century probably), but his nomination is not automatic. He is chosen by an "electoral" college of four dignitaries, presided over by the Prime Minister, the togo naba, as in Ethiopia. He is actually invested with power by the latter who, however, is not a Nakomse (nobleman), but comes from an ordinary family, and who is, in reality, the representative of the people, of all free men, all the citizens who constitute the Mossi nation. The emperor is assisted, in addition to the Prime Minister, by three others; the rassam naba, the balum naba, and the kidiranga naba. Each of them governs one region in addition to his more or less specialized functions. The togo naba is in charge of four royal districts: Tziga, Sissamba, Somniaga, and Bissigai. The togo nabas basically come in turn from three families of commoners residing respectively at Toisi, Kierga, and Node. After the Prime Minister in order of importance comes the rassam naba or bingo naba, chief of the servants of the Crown. He is also the Minister of Finances, guardian of the treasury of precious objects, cowries (coins), bracelets, etc. He is the High Executioner, when occasion arises putting to death condemned criminals. He is chief of the blacksmiths and governs them through interposition of the saba naba. He governs the canton of Kindighi. Therefore, although himself a servant, the rassam naba rules over freemen, and holds power over full-fledged citizens. We will find the same practices among the Wolofs of Cayor Baol and the Serers of Sine Salum in Senegal.

Diop argues that the Mossi Constitution rests on the foundation of the old Ghana Constitution from the first century A.D. This is much earlier than any such constitution in Europe. It should be clear that Diop is not simply trying to show Africa is earlier than Europe on every point. His interested in presenting Africa's own story and when it is presented he sees that it is earlier, more generally extensive, and serves the people well. Nevertheless, this Mossi Constitution is original in certain aspects because the people without royal birth, servants and laborers, were organized into professions or castes, and given representatives within the government. Nothing like this had occurred in the history of the West at this time. Diop is emphatic on this point because he knows the spirit of the Mossi Constitution is unknown in the West. Consider for a moment that around 1352–1353, the time of Ibn Battuta's voyage to the Sudan and the Hundred Years War in Europe, that "the King of France or of England, {gives} a share of his power, with a voice in decisions, to the rural serfs, bound to the soil, the free peasants, the town guildsmen, and the merchants" (Diop, 1987:45). Of course, there is nothing in the history of the West that gives us any indication that this would happen.

The Mossi Constitution was not something that was rare in Africa; it was fundamental to the way many African cultures viewed the world. In fact, the Cayor Constitution also took into account the various types of people in the empire. Accordingly, the government council which invested the king was made of the following titled delegates: Lamane Diamatil, Botal ub Ndiob, and Badie Gateigne, who represented those who were free or had no caste; Eliman of Mballe, Serigne of Kab, who represented the Muslim community; and Dwawerigne MBul Gallo and Diaraf Bunt Ker, who represented the Tieddos and prisoners of the Crown. When the council was convened it was presided over by the Diawerigne MBul Diambur, hereditary representative of free men. The Tieddos were all of those who were attached to the king through military or political service.

Although he makes a strong case for African constitutions, Diop is particularly interested in matrilineal succession, an issue he would revisit in many books and articles, and the concepts of monarchy and royalty as well as the Lebou Republic. He finds an interesting quote from Al-Bakri who visited Ghana in 1067 and wrote of the succession to the kingship in this fashion. He says, "Among this people, custom and rules demand that the successor to the king be his sister's son; for, they say, the sovereign can be sure that his nephew is indeed his sister's son but nothing can assure him that the son he considers his own in actuality is" (Al Bakri, 1913:328).

Among the other topics discussed are political organization, economic organization, ideological superstructure, intellectual and technical levels of society, and migrations of societies. Why is Diop concerned about the African position on these issues before the coming of the European and Arab? I think the answer is quite clear given the history of Diop's engagement with information that seeks to discredit Africans, particularly those traditionally considered Black Africans. He seeks to thrust the position of African cultures prior to colonial experiences as being as rational, organized, and civilized as any in the world. Indeed, since Africa has the oldest cultures, Diop wanted to demonstrate that inherent in the organic political realities of Africans, there was life before the White man. From Diop's point of view it might be that with the coming of the Whites to Africa instead of bringing civilization, which already existed in the place, they brought destruction, degradation, and death.

Precolonial Black Africa is an excellent source for information on the kingdoms of the Sahel. The book, however, does not discuss too many of the Central and Southern African civilizations, such as Zimbabwe, Mapungubwe, and Dhlo Dhlo. It could be said that Diop did not know very much about these cultures because they were outside of his geographical range area. He knew Burkina Faso, Guinea, Chad, Niger, and Mali much more than he knew Nigeria, Angola, Congo, Zimbabwe, and South Africa. Here I do not criticize Diop on this basis. It is impossible for any scholar to know everything about all of the cultures of Africa and every scholar chooses an area of focus. One must use one's own knowledge, languages, and networks to interrogate these cultures. We know, of course, that Diop was most knowledgeable of the Senegal situation vis-à-vis culture and civilization, regardless of the limitations we might recognize with the omission of many of the cultures introduced to the study of pre-colonial Africa.

The major material cultures of Africa appear to have their influences in the same intellectual and philosophical outlook as ancient Egypt. To the degree that scholars can demonstrate this connectiveness, Diop's work is secure as an intellectual advance in our thinking. If it were possible to disprove the connection of the civilizations of Africa, it would have already been done. But Diop insured his work would last by providing his readers with enormous evidences from many sources. In my opinion, the link between Kemet, Nubia, Axum, Ghana, Mali, Songhay, Mossi, Zimbabwe, Chokwe, Swahili, and Mapungubwe has been established by Diop and his students in many publications can be seen as in the African tradition. What is more is that the groundwork has been laid to examine how cultures that have not been explored in relationship to each other can be seen as in the African tradition. What are the key characteristics one ought to be looking for in investigating the symbiotic nature of these cultural relationships?

When Diop wrote *Cultural Unity of Black Africa*, there was a need to re-assert the commonalities between the cultures. The evidence had been coming in from all over the continent that casual investigations had yielded similar responses to the environment and to governance among Africans but that we had not adequately processed the information. We were essentially the same people, with similar outlooks on life, but because of colonialism we had come to view African cultures as being quite dissimilar to each other. Diop steps up to the plate, so to speak, and says listen to your own voices. In this light the work of the African American linguist Lorenzo Turner becomes important because he established the fact that hundreds of words used in American English were African words. Turner was not equipped to make comparisons between groups of African languages. This would be some of the work to be taken up by Diop and his students.

Although Diop did not teach at the University, students came to him for lectures and advice and this is where the cultural unity idea first appeared. Diop reasoned the next level of assault on the Western paradigm about Africa was to question the thesis that Africa was hopelessly divided. He argued that there was a strong basis for cultural unity that stretched to the classical civilizations. This was not to be a challenge thrown out, but a demonstration using several main principles of culture while concentrating on the matrilineal idea. He was the best person to attempt this because he had read the anthropologists and historians on the issue of African philosophy, religion and culture.

GENERAL ASSUMPTIONS
ABOUT LANGUAGE AND CULTURE

The evidence in Diop's work of linguistic relationships is overwhelming. There is almost no evidence so pointed and so powerful as the impact of showing, as he had done at Cairo, the correspondences between ancient Egyptian language, Wolof and Coptic, or any other correspondences between languages. What he operates on is the basic idea that there is a steady stream of cultural artifacts that connect African people through language. He argues on the basis of these assumptions:

1. There can be no coherent understanding of African contributions to science without a reconnection in every conceivable way of the Nile Valley Complex (Kemet, Nubia, Axum) to the rest of Africa,
2. All discussions of African languages must begin with a re-assessment of non-African categorizations of African languages, and
3. The interpretation of African languages must rest on etymological plausibility correlated with other aspects of African cultural behavior

In *Precolonial Black Africa*, Diop (1987) used ethnonyms to chart the migrations of African people in West Africa. And in *The African Origin of Civilization*, Diop (1974:182–183) used "analyses acculturaliste" or typological analysis to study the origin and spread of African cultural features from the Nile Valley to West Africa through his examination of toponyms (Diop, 1974, 182–183). In the *Cultural Unity of Black Africa*, Diop (1960) discussed, among other factors, the common totems and religious practices many African ethnic groups share. The totemic nature of most African societies harks back to the ancient Egyptian classical system. Diop understood this and made a point of suggesting that one could find similar attitudes and beliefs in all contemporary African nations. As Diop (1989:172) says of African culture, "Every family has its totemic name, that of its mythical ancestor, of its clan, of its genos, so to speak, but with a matrilineal base." Thus, he emphasizes again that among the Europeans everything gravitated around the father to symbolize the patrilineal descent and the patrilineal regime. This was not the case with African culture which remained matrilineal until the encounters with Arabs and Europeans in this era. This is an area that is yet to be fully explored inasmuch as the connection with Native American populations and other peoples throughout the world can be made. It appears that only Europe is devoid of a totemic nature.

Diop finds other interesting aspects to the unity of African culture. Indeed, he argues that Africans bury their dead which is an indication to him of the southern cradle of civilization in contradistinction from the northern cradle, the cradle of the nomads, where one finds the worship of fire, the cremation of the dead. He reasons from this fact that the southern cradle had retained its sedentary way of life and the importance of the ancestors, being in place, was a matter of religion. For him (1987:34),

It is within the framework of sedentary life that the existence of the tomb can be justified. Thus it is impossible to find any trace of the practice of cremation in an agricultural land such as Africa from antiquity to the present day. All of the cases mentioned are unauthentic; they are only the suppositions of researchers in whose minds the demarcation between the two cradles is not clear and who, referring to the Northern cradle, tend to identify any trace of fire as a vestige of cremation, even when no religious objects can be found nearby. The practice of cremation was also unknown in ancient Egypt.

Fire ceremonies of all types have been popular in Europe since the prehistoric times giving rise to Diop's argument for cremation among nomadic people. In societies, such as one often finds among Native American Indians, in Mexico and the United States, where the ruling classes were cremated while the masses were buried one gets the idea that this harks back to the time when a ruling warrior, nomadic dynasty conquered a population of sedentary people and preserved their practice to cremation. Although tombs are known in Africa and people visit tombs to pour libations, to pray, and to show respect, "nowhere in Africa does there exist this multitude of domestic altars surmounted by sacred fires which must be kept burning as long as the family exists, a custom which seems to stem directly from the Northern worship of fire" (Diop, 1989:35).

Clearly Diop knows African and European history and his interrogation of the fire cultures of Europe is based upon evidence from Europeans themselves. Fire worship is pre-eminently a Northern phenomenon because the god benefactor of the far Northern climes is fire. Those latitudes found fire to be indispensable and so "the primitive Northern soul was not long in coming to worship it" (Diop, 1989:46). Unquestionably cremation and fire worship arise from a strictly Indo-European tradition. It has no parallel in the customs and mores of African people. And while the origins of the tradition are often forgotten by the European people who practice the tradition of cremation it has perpetuated itself in the consciousness of the people by ideas like the everlasting flame, the Olympic torch, the cremation of Christians. Diop (Ibid.) opines that, "It is likely that certain Europeans would not allow themselves to be cremated today, even for reasons of hygiene, were it not for this tradition handed down from their Aryan ancestors. It is remarkable to observe that cremation is the ethnological and cultural trait which distinguishes the Aryan world from the Southern world, and in particular from the African one. It is impossible to identify a single authentic case of cremation in Black Africa, from antiquity to the present day. This is a fact which has never been sufficiently stressed."

There is little doubt that Diop knows that his method of investigation which is Afrocentric yields enormous rewards. He is a master at following the course of language itself even when he is trying to discover support for an opposing view. Thus, he finds that the European writers have not been able to find a single example where there has been the phenomenon of ossification of consanguinity "over a period of 4000 years" that was similar to that claimed for the Hawaiians. It was claimed that the Hawaiian family underwent living changes but while the system of consanguinity ossifies the system survives by the force or custom. The family outgrows it. He (1989:40) writes that "the sacred character of the mother in the societies which are sedentary, agricultural and matriarchal is ill-suited to the idea of a primitive stage of promiscuous intercourse which they are said to have passed through. Where this latter has existed, it seems to have led directly to amazons, which must not be confused with matriarchy."

Cheikh Anta Diop is wedded to the idea that an investigation of the languages of Africa will reveal enormous cultural wealth. In writing of Diop's appreciation for this possibility I am reminded that the Kenyan Ngugi wa Thiong'o and the Ghanaian Ayi Kwei Armah have made similar pleas for the critical study and use of African languages. There is no question that this is going to be the frontier of future research in Africa since the documentable texts are scarce. We could learn a lot from following this line. For Diop one could consider a common physical type and a common cultural pattern as significant in establishing the idea of cultures that might have genetically related languages. Diop seeks to advance the idea that onomastics, comparative linguistics, and semantics might enlighten the relatedness of African cultures (Diagne, 1981). Onomastics is the science of discovering in names certain cultural and social forms and identities. For example, one could see in the Twi name, "Mensa", a correspondence with the Egyptian "Amen Sa" or "sa Amen," giving the rendering "the son of Amen" or "the son of God." There are many examples that need to be explored and studied alongside other evidences in the languages. It goes without saying that European writers have made much more of the connections and correspondences in their languages to the ancient Greek and Latin terms than African scholars have.

Diop (1988:12) cautions us that we do not have an adequate appreciation or understanding of the Egyptian lexical repository to be able to make a definitive survey of the Egyptian language. As he writes pointedly, "It can also be emphasized that the Egyptians—no more than any other ancient people—had never prepared an academic dictionary and that consequently the vocabulary collected according to the texts is necessarily fragmentary. It therefore often happened that Egyptian expression which have not been certified survived in related African languages; but only further systematic investigations will make this point of view sufficiently conclusive." Here is a cautious researcher, one who knows that something is missing but who is unwilling to venture beyond that for which he can offer adequate evidence. This was always what distinguished Diop from those who sought to challenge his work. Unquestionably our ancient Egyptian vocabulary, the one that we teach our students, is derived from extant Kemetic texts. We have no knowledge of how many words do not appear in the texts that we have at our disposal.

One of the key interests in Diop's construction of Africa as a unity was to see how the naming process aided in the convergence of political and social ideas. It was possible, he believed, to examine myths, legends, the name of places, and religious terminology in order to reveal the hidden depth of African typonymy and ethnonymy (Diop, 1978:67). What he knew was that the origin of civilization in antiquity was along the Nile River valley. If typonymy or ethnonymy could assist in identifying how Africans saw their world it would be a logical ideal for African scholars to explore in depth the meaning of words, names, and terms. Diop (1981:86) observed that: "An undisputed linguistic relationship between two geographically remote groups of languages can be relevant for the study of migrations. A grammatical (or genetic) relationship if clear enough is never an accident." To ascertain relationship, Diop used toponyms (place-names), anthroponyms (personal names) and ethnonyms (names of ethnic groups) as evidence of analogous ethnic (clan) names in West Africa and the Upper Nile (Diop, 1991).

In *Precolonial Black Africa*, Diop used ethnonyms to chart the migrations of African people in West Africa. And in *The African Origin of Civilization*, Diop used typological analysis to study the dissemination of African cultural features from the Nile Valley to West Africa (Diop, 1974, 182–183). In the *Cultural Unity of Black Africa*, he (1978:124) discussed the common totems and religious terms shared by various ethnic groups. Cheikh Anta Diop was a major proponent of comparative linguistics of the African continent. He understood it as a sound method for examining African culture. In as much as linguistic taxonomy is the foundation for comparative and historical linguistics (Ruhlen, 1994) the Diopian method would try to determine language families through linguistic taxonomy. Although there is always room for doubt when one tries to show direct contribution it is possible to show a pattern of regular sound correspondences in order to reconstruct a proto-language (Hock, 1988; Crawley, 1992; Bynon, 1978; Lord, 1966; Robins, 1974).

Diop was keen enough to see that linguistic resemblances often denote historical relationship although it is sometimes difficult to say how long ago that relationship existed. What we can say, and what Diop would have argued, is that resemblances in fundamental vocabulary can help us reconstruct the culture of the speakers of genetically related languages. Diop (1989:1) wrote in the introduction to *Cultural Unity of Black Africa*:

> I have tried to bring out the profound cultural unity still alive beneath the deceptive appearance of cultural heterogeneity. It would be inexcusable for one led by chance to experience deeply the living reality of the land not to try to furnish knowledge of the African sociological actuality.

There is a strong commitment in Diop to work for the reclamation of African experiences as valid contributions to human civilization. But even more, he is interested in showing how the cultural unity of Africa is at the door to the revitalization of the continent. If it had not been for the European people insisting on their cultural patterns and styles, Africans would not have questioned the unity that existed among the cultures. Underneath the façade of differences were the same basic responses to the environment that established the idea of cultural unity.

Thus, Diop establishes the principles of matriarchy and patriarchy as buttressed by matrilineality and patrilineality in order to contend that the African culture is essentially a matrilineal one. He demonstrates the patrilineality of the European culture and shows how this plays out in the lives and behaviors of the people. Diop argues that humanity has been divided into two camps, matriarchy and patriarchy. This split happened soon after the human migration out of Africa into Europe. Combating the authors who argue that patriarchy is an evolutionary superior state to matriarchy, Diop (1989:19) argues for two cradles, one that was favorable to the flourishing of matriarchy and the other that was profitable for the establishment of patriarchy.

Always the scholar seeking to be thorough in his analysis, Diop first examines the roots of Europe's insistence on the superiority of patriarchy by re-reading the classical texts in the area. For example, he analyzes the work of J. J. Bachofen, Henry Lewis Morgan, and F. Engels to show that they had made some important mistakes in their construction of the evolution of the family. According to Diop, J. J. Bachofen (1861) published the book, *Das Mutterrecht*, as the first work on the subject. Morgan (1871) followed with another volume on the subject which he called *Systems of Consanguinity and Affinity*. This work confirmed the research that had been made by Bachofen. Then in 1884, Friedrich Engels used the discoveries of Bachofen and Morgan to develop his own response to the question of the family. His work, *The Origin of the Family, Private Property and the State* (1972), produced the first work out of the socialist school on the subject. All three of these works elevated patriarchy.

Diop admits that he is following the account of Bachofen theory from the work of Adrien Turel who wrote *Du Regne de la Mere au Patriarchie* (From the Rule of the Mother to Patriarchy). At the time of Diop's work, Turel's volume was the only work in French on the subject. Nevertheless, he is keen to provide the fullest account possible of what Bachofen said. Diop (1989:5–6) states that:

> Bachofen considers that mankind in its earliest states underwent a period of barbarism and sexual promiscuity, so that descent could only be reckoned through the female line. All paternal descent being doubtful. Marriage did not exist.
>
> A second stage, called the gynaecocratic, follows on the first as its logical sequel. It is characterized by marriage and the supremacy of the woman; descent is still reckoned following the female line as during the previous period. This is the real age of matriarchy according to BachofenAmazonism is equally characteristic of this age. Finally, there comes a third stage, distinguished from the others by a new form of marriage under the domination of the male, by masculine imperialism: this is the reign of patriarchy.

What is so brilliant in Diop's understanding of this position is that he uses his own location, that is, cultural location and sense of African history to interrogate what he reads. This is a useful technique for all readers from oppressed and conquered societies. He realizes almost instanteously that something is not right with Bachofen's formulation of the evolutionary history of the family. Indeed, Bachofen sees a universal movement for matriarchy to patriarchy; the idea is that human beings gave up one form, matriarchy, for another, patriarchy. The first form was inferior, the second form was superior. Diop understood that one could go on from here to make negative comments about those societies where matriarchy still existed, in fact, those societies appeared to be the majority around the world. Yet Bachofen was confident that he had defined the progress of the human race on the basis of patriarchy being the highest end of the family trail.

With this information in the hands of Cheikh Anta Diop the entire enterprise becomes one of demonstrating once again how the Europeans had falsified the records and made enormous mistakes due to their racism. For example, it was Morgan who argued that the identification of the totemic clans of the American Indians must be seen as an argument for the primacy of the totemic clans. In fact, the genos of the Greeks and the gens of the Romans are directly related to the totems. According to Diop (Ibid:11), Morgan established that ". . . it was the Indian forms of social organization which are the more ancient and that the Greco-Latin forms are derived from them." So now we have Morgan arriving at the same conclusion as Bachofen that matriarchy is universal and that it has at one time governed all people.

Of course, what this means is that these two authors have established that patriarchy is not the earliest form of family. This is important for Engels, who as a Marxist, wanted to show that all forms of political or social organization are temporary. He could contend that the traditional monogamous bourgeois family was not a permenet form and that it would be stricken by decay as all previous forms. Thus, even the Marxists relied upon the arguments that had been made by previous writers who insisted on the progression from matriarchy to patriarchy. The real issue in this discussion, however, must be the fact that although Bachofen and Morgan have made some researches and have advanced ideas of the evolution from matriarchy to patriarchy, they have made some major errors. Diop is ready to seize upon these errors almost immediately. As a scholar, he had presented their positions with clarity and generosity, giving credit to their dedicated research where it was necessary but also showing that there were flaws.

One of the first criticisms of the theory of universal matriarchy is that it has not been demonstrated that matriarchy is everywhere the same, that is, that in antiquity all societies went through it. Diop (Ibid:21) makes an entirely logical point when he writes of Bachofen's position:

> The demonstration of a universal transition from matriarchy to patriarchy is only scientifically acceptable if it can be proved that this internal evolution has definitely taken place among a specific people. Now this condition has never been fulfilled in the works of the author. It has never been possible to determine the existence of a historical period during which the Greeks and the Romans might have lived under matriarchy.

Pointing out the problematic way the European writers had constructed their argument for a classical universal matriarchy, Diop then shows how these European scholars got around this issue of Greek and Roman matriarchy. They went to aboriginal people that they found on the spot at the time that these people were becoming sedentary. Indeed, these people were the same ones that were being destroyed by the Whites as representatives of an alien people, an alien culture, and different people.

Cheikh Anta Diop knew how to finish his point with a flourish once he got an inside track on his opposition. Here he (Ibid:21) has an inside track and says,

> it is therefore necessary to go back to the time of the Etruscans, who were completely destroyed by the Romans, in order to show the existence of matriarchy in Italy. Now, nothing is more doubtful than the gynacocracy of Etruscans. . . . When discussing the Athenians, the factors justifying the existence of matriarchy must be sought among the Pelasgians.

In the end, the theory of Bachofen is anti-scientific because "it is unlikely that such geographically different cradles as the Eurasian steppes-favorable to a nomadic life—and the Southern regions of the globe and in particular Africa—favorable to agriculture and a sedentary way of life—could have produced the same type of social organization" (Ibid: 21–22). He (Ibid: 22) is convinced that "this criticism gains in importance if the influence of environment on social and political forms is admitted. In supposing that matriarchy originated in the South and patriarchy in the North, that the former preceded the latter in the Mediterranean basin, and that in Western Asia both systems were supermimposed on each other in certain regions, the hypothesis of a universal transition from one to the other ceases to be necessary." All issues of status of women, modes of inheritance, and consanguinity can be explained in other ways.

EXAMPLES FROM THE TWO CRADLES

Diop's thesis is provocative, but it is based on science. He contends that if you go back into European history only one form of social organization occurs, as far as linguistic analysis is concerned, and that is a common nomadic tradition. Diop explores the longevity of words for horse, sheep, and cattle in several European languages and then concludes that the Indo-Europeans towards the end of the common life, were a people of shepherds, sheep and cattle-raisers, and were probably semi-nomadic because they had to be mobile. Even the classical writers Diodorus Siculus and Herodotus say that the Scythian's house is his wagon. There is "no generic term denoting the word "city" in the primitive foundation of the vocabulary" (Ibid: 23). Diop quotes Aymard at length on the lack of a word for city. In fact, there is an expression in the early Aryan languages for "fortified place" but not for city. What would become the word used for "city" in the future would be the words that had been used for fortifications, thus, the Greek *polis*, or the Sanskrit *pur*, or the Lithuanian *pilis*. Also, the German city, Frankfort, carries with it the designation of fortification.

The role of women in these early European societies was one of great suffering. The woman was often reduced to child-bearing because in the world of nomads there was no economic value to the woman. Indeed, "she was only a burden that the man dragged behind him" (Ibid: 23). Considerable energy must have gone into the process of keeping women down in such a society. Contrary to the matriarchy form, it is the woman who must leave her clan and join that of her husband. It is well known that

> among the Greeks, the Romans and the Aryans of India, the woman who leaves her own *genos* to join her husband's *gens* becomes attached to the latter and can no longer inherit from her own; she has broken with the natural family, in the eyes of which she is no more than a stranger. She can no longer take part in the family worship, without which no relationship is possible; she must even compensate for her economic inferiority by the dowry she

brings to her husband. The latter has the right of life and death over her; he is not answerable to the state in regard to the lot to which he can submit her."

So it is in this way that Diop lays the foundation to discuss the two cradle theory. It is not a unreasoned theory that seeks to divide the world into two, but rather a scientific analysis of the political and social organizations that have made our contemporary world. After a considerable treatment of the various ways in which the Southern, or Meridional Cradle, differs from the Northern Cradle, Diop writes a succinct conclusion.

> The Meridional Cradle, confined to the African continent in particular, is characterized by the matrilineal family, the creation of the territorial state, in contrast to the Aryan city-state, the emancipation of woman in domestic life, xenophilia, cosmo-politanism, a sort of social collectivism having as a corollary a tranquility going as far as unconcern for tomorrow, a material solidarity of right for each individual, which makes moral or material misery unknown to the present day; there are people living in poverty, but no one feels alone and no one is in distress. In the moral domain, it shows an ideal of peace, of justice, of goodness and an optimism which eliminates all notion of guilt or original sin in religious and metaphysical institutions. The types of literature most favoured are the novel, tales, fables and comedy.
>
> The Northern cradle, confined to Greece and Rome, is characterized by the patriarchal family, by the city-state (there was between two cities, said Fustel de Coulanges, something more impassable than a mountain); it is easily seen that it is on contact with the southern world that the Northerners broadened their conception of the state, elevating themselves to the idea of a territorial state and of an empire. The particular character of these city-states,

outside of which a man was an outlaw, developed an internal patriotism, as well as xenophobia. Individualism, moral and material solitude, a disgust for existence, all the subject-matter of modern literature, which even in its philosophic aspects is none other than the expression of the tragedy of a way of life going back to the Aryans' ancestors, are all attributes of this cradle. An ideal of war, violence, crime and conquests, inherited from nomadic life, with as a consequence, a feeling of guilt and of original sin, which causes pessimistic religious or metaphysical systems to be built, is the special attribute of this cradle.

This is how Diop conceived the two cradles. Unfortunately his critics have not read his work closely and have made all types of mistakes in criticism. As you can see, Diop is a careful scholar and his words are measured. He has reflected on the nature of the two cradles and found something entirely different in them. This is not to say that there are not individual examples of overlaps or some exceptional cases, but taken together his words represent the best presentation of the wisdom collected from experience, science, history and philosophy. He also argues that because of many modernizing factors it is difficult for the West to imagine what the enslavement of women was like under the patriarchal regime. In addition, the literary style preferred by the Northern cradle is tragedy or drama as contrasted with the African cultural interest in the cosmic drama.

AFRICAN ORIGIN OF GREEK WORDS

There is another way to examine African languages as well. One does not simply have to look for patterns of correspondences. It is possible that one can look for patrimony of terms and see that certain words in one language are derived from another. Numerous

Greek words are derived from African words. In fact, the presence of African words in the Greek language of the European classical age suggests the greater antiquity of the African classical ages. Greek, as a relatively new language during the 6th and 5th centuries B.C.E, used an eclectic source for many of its terms. And Egyptian, or Kemetic, words added significantly to the Greek language. In this section I am concerned with only a few of the words found in a discussion of the etymology of classical Greek vocabulary. Thus, syntax, semantics, and grammar are not addressed in this work. By omitting these elements, I do not imply that Africa did not impact the mode of thinking of Greece. It undoubtedly did, as we know from the many works of Theophile Obenga, Cheikh Anta Diop, Charles Finch, and many other historians and philosophers.

In a recent doctoral dissertation on Egyptian influences on Greek philomythy, Leophus Tarharka King, Jr. (2004) demonstrated a close relationship between the ancient Egyptian and Greek languages in the area of creation mythology. The Greek myths of creation bear what King calls "imprints" and "trails" related to the ancient African construction of myths. What he did as a Diopian project was to draw out the principal markers of the ancient On and Men-nefer creation myths and see how they corresponded to the Greek myths. It was unbelievable to the researcher to have found so many correspondences that he concluded the Greek myths, which were more recent, had to have been influenced in some way by the much older Egyptian myths.

My aim is more modest. I simply want to begin a process of discovering the etymology of the Greek words and see how Africa contributed to the enrichment of Greek language. We know from several sources that seven-eights of the 4100 words used in the Greek language from Homer to Plato are really compound words. Many of these compounds are derived from other languages and of those from other languages, many come from ancient Egyptian.

Liddell and Scott's *Lexicon* deals effectively with the Greek language in its classical dimensions but does not provide an orientation toward African sources. The same can be said about E. R. Whartons's *Etymological Lexicon of Classical Greek* (1974). However, Wharton does present us with sources for Greek words which are useful for this illustration: For example, the following words (English translations) are of Egyptian derivation: *board, porridge, boat, fox, papyrus-bark, vulture, wine, beer, cloth, bird, leather cloak, beetle, monkey, castor oil plant, palm, lotus, gum, spelt-bread, plant, truffle, papyrus, salted perch,* and *tree.*

LINGUISTICS CLASSIFICATIONS AND RATES OF CHANGE

Cheikh Anta Diop's emphasis on archaeology must be looked at in connection with his emphasis on linguistics. He believed that language was an important means of demonstrating the relationship of one people to another and could find in Africa, among the Peul, for example, a relationship to the ancient language of Egypt. This was not unusual for him. It was not to be seen as something unexpected, but something that was organic to the makeup of Africa itself.

J. H. Greenberg (1963), in his work, *The Languages of Africa,* attempted to identify all African language groups. This led to a major controversy among African scholars themselves. In fact, neither Diop nor Theophile Obenga (Obenga, 1992) agrees with Greenberg's classifications. Greenberg spoke of four broad areas: Afro-asiatic, Nilo-Saharan, Congo-Kordofanian, and Khoisan. The Afro-asiatic includes Arabic, Amharic, Gurage, Tigrinya, Berber, Tuareg, Tamaschek, Somali, Galla, Afar, Sidamo, Beja, Fali, and Hausa. The Nilo-Saharan includes Acholi, Shilluk, Mangbetu, Kanuri, Teda, Zaghawa, and Songhai. The Congo-Kordofanian includes Dyola, Fulani, Temne, Mwa, Mende, Mossi, Dogon, Talensi, Ibo, Akan, Bini, Yoruba, Shona, Xhosa, Kongo, Gikuyu, and Igala. Khoisan includes !Kung,

Nama, Sandawe, and Hadza. Greenberg added main divisions to each of the four broad language families. Both Diop and Obenga have challenged Greenberg's classification of African languages. Obenga, following the Diopian tradition, is adamant that Greenberg has made a major error in classification.

As Clyde Winter has written Diop appreciated the variability of language, the rate of linguistic change, and the cultural context of language development. It goes without saying that the rate of increase in the linguistic change in a community depends upon a lot of factors that may relate to economics and cultural activities. Diop knew this and worked to explain his theories of language and linguistic correspondences by suggesting that Western scholars had distorted the nature of African languages. Pathe Diagne has suggested that the way Europe looks at language is based on the development of language in Europe. The Western scholars infer that the European pattern is universal when they say that the rate of change for all languages is both rapid and constant (Diagne, 1981:238). What is valid for Europe is not necessarily valid for all the languages of the world. It is believed by a number of writers that African languages change much slower than European languages (Armstrong, 1962). We know, for example, that African words collected by Arab explorers more than a thousand years ago are comparable to contemporary lexical items (Diagne, 1981:239). Of course, what Cheikh Anta Diop believed and what other African scholars proved is that there are striking resemblances between the ancient Egyptian language and Coptic, and between Pharonic Egyptian and African languages (Diagne, 1981; Diop, 1977; Obenga, 1988, 1992a, 1992b, 1993).

My thesis has always been that the political stability of the African states and kingdoms prior to the interaction with the Europeans and Arabs meant that the societies changed little and therefore languages changed little. Clyde Winters (1994) has made a similar argument. I would add, however, that the ancient empire of Ghana lasted for

66

nearly 1500 years, a considerable period of time given the brevity of most nations and kingdoms. This meant that the organizational structure, the infrastructure of institutions, and the rituals and ceremonies of culture in the kingdom were repeated over and over without much interruption. Generations came and went and the languages remain essentially the same. Although Pawley and Ross (1993) argue that a sedentary life style may be responsible for some of the constancy of African languages or any languages, I am inclined to believe that it is rather the political stability that causes a people to retain their concepts and values and indeed the language that speaks to those concepts and values (Diop, 1987, 1991; Niane, 1984).

I am convinced that Diop appreciated the fact that African languages changed more slowly than European languages and therefore gave rise to correspondences over a wide geographical territory although many of the languages come from different roots. Diop (1974:153–154) wrote that:

> First the evolution of languages, instead of moving everywhere at the same rate of speed seems linked to other factors; such as, the stability of social organizations or the opposite, social upheavals. Understandably in relatively stable society's, man's language has changed less with the passage of time.

Furthermore, he (1988:17) wrote in *Nouvelles recherches sur l'egyptien ancien et les langues négro-africaine modernes* that: "The permanence of these forms not only, constitute today a solid base . . . upon which . . . [we are to re-construct diachronic African languages], but obliges also a radical revision of these ideas, a priori . . . on the evolution of these languages in general."

Cheikh Anta Diop theorized that the permanence of linguistic forms might assist African scholars, particularly his cadre of dedicated researchers in the service of Africa, in discovering the connections that demonstrate how West African languages and other languages in the continent were related to the Nile Valley civilizations, the classical languages. Armstrong (1962) had mentioned the fact that there was evidence of linguistic continuity of African languages when he used glottochronology to test the rate of change in Yoruba. Armstrong used the Yoruba words collected by Koelle nearly one hundred and thirty years earlier to compare with modern Yoruba words. He found little internal or external modifications in the lexical items.

No one knew more than Cheikh Anta Diop that language as a social practice and a historical institution would constitute one of the principal loci of discourse around the African origin of ancient Egypt, or to put it in Diop's own way of speaking, the Black African origin of Pharaonic civilization. One could study the changes in a society by looking at how the language changed. Indeed, one could tell from the rapidity of changes what was going on in the society in terms of political shifts and changes. The language of the government, whatever the government, often becomes the language of the society. It remains an adage that ruling classes are the definers of ruling languages and it was necessary for a researcher to plumb the dense fields of language in order to make sense of the African past.

One of Diop's major linguistic contributions has been the classification and re-classification of African languages. In this he has been followed by some of his greatest disciples including Obenga (1988, 1993b), Anselin (1989, 1992b) and Winters (1985, 1986, 1989). Beginning with a general interest in correspondences Diop began to examine morphological and phonological similarities between Egyptian and other Black African languages. In *Parentè gènètique de l'Egyptien Pharaonique et des languues Negro-Africaines* (1977) Diop explained the phonological rules of the Egyptian and other African languages. It was the works of Anselin and Obenga that pushed the limits on this analysis and gave other researchers a reason to advance the intellectual question of African unity. For his part, Diop made inferences from ethnic customs and behaviors and explored the possibility that one could go into the past by interrogating other than documented records. One could see how people buried their dead or ask questions about the core use of ritual language. All things were open to the African researcher intent on putting right the past that had been badly mauled by White scholarship.

One of the advantages that he suggested was that linguistic correspondences could assist us in making inferences about culture itself. Following this line of thinking, Obenga (1988) sought to reconstruct the Paleo-African terms for cattle, goat, sheep, rams and the monkey. How did the Africans in different parts of the continent call these animals? Are there evidences of traces of these original proto-typical lexical items in the languages of West and Central Africa?

Diop has contributed much to the extra-African linguistic relationship. He was a major proponent of the Dravidian-African relationship (Diop, 1974:116), and he illustrated the African substratum in Indo-European languages in relationship to cacuminal sounds and terms for social organization and culture (1974:115). Diop (1978:113) also recognized that in relation to Arabic words, after the suppression of the first consonant, there is often an African root. This is not surprising because Edward Wilmot Blyden (1887) found evidence that the Arabic writing system was created by an African from the modern country we call Egypt (Bangura, 2000).

Theophile Obenga has taken on the mantle of Diop (1974, 1978, 1995). Obenga is a linguist and historian. He has done remarkable work in the reconstruction of Paleo-African and a brilliant study of the philosophical views of the Egyptians. This is not all that Obenga has done; he is in many ways much like Diop in his intellectual reach. An early major work of Obenga was *L'Afrique dans l'Antiquitie*. In this book Obenga discussed the African origin of Egypt and the cultural and linguistic unity of Blacks world wide. Obenga (1978a, 1978b, 1988) has shown the unity of ancient and modern African languages and the close relationship of ancient Egyptian to his own language Mbochi. And in *The Peopling of Ancient Egypt and the Decipherment of the Meroitic Script*, Obenga and Diop give a superb discussion of the reality of an African origin of Egyptian civilization.

Obenga (1978b, 1988) concentrates on two areas of linguistic research. First, he has shown striking affinities between Egyptian and Mbochi. Secondly, Obenga (1988, 1993) has been concerned with the reconstruction of Paleo-African and the shared grammatical features of Egyptian and Black African languages. The middle nineties were immensely full of activity for the scholars committed to the advance of African cultural interpretations. Theophile Obenga, the Congolese scholar, published *Origine commune de l'egyptien ancien du copte et des langues negro africaines modernes* (1993) to demonstrate the linkage that existed between Egyptian language and other African languages. He believed that there were three

superfamilies of African language: the Black African-Egyptian, the Berber, and the Khoisan languages. These are the only divisions that make most sense to the Afrocentric Egyptologists. What is also important to note is that Obenga classifies the subfamilies of the Egyptian-Black African Family as consisting of the following languages: Egyptian, Cushitic, Tchadian, Nilo-Saharan and the Niger-Kordofanian families. In addition, Obenga offers proof that the Egyptian language is closer in construction and phonology to African languages than to the non-African languages grouped by Greenberg in the Afro-Asiatic family of languages. Tounkara (1989) suggested that it is more logical to see a connection between Egyptian and other Black African languages because of social and historical evidence than to try to support an Afro-Asiatic hypothesis which usually includes Arabia, Syria, Iraq, Israel, and other parts of Southwest Asia as well as Africa.

Other scholars have come forth to argue for correspondence between the Bantu, Duala and the ancient Egyptian language. This work has been done by Gilbert Ngom (1986) who also elaborates on a discussion of Black African-Egyptian phonology suggesting that Egyptian is closer to other Black African languages than it is to Berber and Semitic languages in syntax, morphology and phonology (Ngom, 1986:48–52). Anselin (1989, 1993) provides argument for the affinity between Egyptian and other Black African verbal systems. The linguistic data gathered and analyzed by Alain Anselin (1989, 1992a, 1993) and Oscar Pfouma (1993) have been used to show that Black African and Egyptian terms referring to royalty and religion have a strong correspondence. Clyde Ahmad Winters (1985, 1989) was one of the earliest scholars to probe the links suggested by Diop. He has gone further to examine Asian correspondences and has argued for a relationship between the African, the Dravidian, the Elamite and the Sumerian languages. Anselin (1982:190) and other scholars have shown an interest in demonstrating the relationship between African languages and those of East Asia. This has opened up the discourse on the influence of Africa in numerous ways. One has to look to Diop for influence in this style of research.

It is often said that linguistic analysis was at the root of Diop's Afrocentric historical method. I believe that this is the case with most of his work. The Diopian view of historiography combines the research of linguistics, history and psychology to interpret the cultural unity of African people. His fundamental approach to all historical subjects was through the interrogation of language, although he used many other techniques. In many ways, it is probably true that Diop, more than Du Bois, built the foundations for an Afrocentric understanding of history. Writing in *Precolonial Black Africa* about a center of dispersal around the Nile Valley to the rest of Africa, Diop (1987:213) says, "By an investigative method using linguistic, ethnological, and toponymic data, we will try to bring out, in a practically certain manner, the origins of the Laobe, Tuklor, Peul, Yoruba, Agni, Serer, and other people." There is not one method to gain the knowledge that is necessary to reconstruct the Black past; the researcher must use all of the tools at his or her disposal. This is the lesson of Diop.

Even his strong contention for toponymic evidence shows that he is attuned to many cultures in Africa. For example, he (Ibid:215) states that:

> It must be recalled that Kandaka (Candace), the name, or rather the title, of the queens of the Sudan, beginning with the time of Augustus Ceasar, was also borne by the first kings of Kau (Gao), according to Al Bakri; they were called Kanda. The women of this region, according to the same author, in the tenth century, wore wigs such as those worn in Egypt and Nubia. In antiquity there was a Nubian nome called Kau, the exact location of which has not been identified, according to Budge. The inhabitants of Upper Egypt were called Kau-Kau in the Egyptian tongue. We know that Gao is both an abbreviation and a deformation of the real name of that city: Kau-Kau. Inhabitants of the interior of Senegal even today have the name of Kau-Kau (Cayor, Baol), which those of the coast, as in ancient Libya, are called Lebou: They are the fishermen of the whole region of the Niaye (coastal palm forest).

Diop's method is multidimensional and this allows him to look for evidence and correspondences outside of written documents; he engages a wide range of sources. If scholars could learn one thing from his method it would be to thoroughly interrogate life (Mazama, 2003).

This linguistic research has been based on linguistic classification or taxonomy. Linguistic taxonomy is the foundation upon which comparative and historical linguistic methods are based (Ruhlen, 1994). Linguistic taxonomy is necessary for the identification of language families. The determination of language families gives us the material to reconstruct the proto-language of a people and discover regular sound correspondences.

There are three major kinds of language classifications: genealogical, typological, and areal. A genealogical classification groups languages together into language families based on the shared features retained by languages since divergence from the common ancestor or proto-language. A typological classification groups languages together into language types by the similarity in the appearance of the structure of languages without consideration of their historical origin and present, or past geographical distribution. An areal classification groups languages into linguistic areas based on shared features acquired by a process of convergence arising from spatial proximity.

Unquestionably it is Cheikh Anta Diop's knowledge of languages that has made him such an important force in African civilization. Diop (1977:xxv) once wrote:

> The process for the evolution of African languages is clearly apparent; from afar we (have) the idea that Wolof is descendant by direct filiation to ancient Egyptian, but the Wolof, Egyptian and other African languages (are) derived from a common mother language that one can call Paleo-African, the common mother language that one can call Paleo-African, the common African or the Negro-African of L. Homburger or of Th. Obenga.

The Africological method of linguistic analysis has as its objective the reconstruction of African cultural behaviors and styles so that we may see connections with other Africans and therefore restore a sense of unity. There are two aspects of this objective: (1) establish the history of language families and show the relatedness between African languages, and (2) reconstruct the mother language to determine where languages diverged. In general, comparative linguists are interested in determining phonetic laws, analogy/correspondence and loan words. It is certainly true that

Diop was a strong supporter of the comparative method in the rediscovery of Paleo-African. The reconstruction of Paleo-African involves both reconstruction and recognition of regular sound correspondence. The goal of reconstruction is the discovery of the proto-language of African people is the recovery of Paleo-African:

(1) vowels and consonants
(2) specific Paleo-African words
(3) common grammatical elements; and
(4) common syntactic elements.
(5) common royal titles of queens and kings

The comparative method is useful in the reconstruction of Proto-languages or Diop's Paleo-African. To reconstruct a proto-language the linguist must look for *patterns of correspondences* in order to discover terms which show uniformity. This uniformity leads to the inference that languages are related since conformity of terms in two or more languages indicate they came from a common ancestor.

Since language gives us evidence of a person's cultural elements, then it is the reconstruction of Paleo-African terms that can help us make inferences about a group's culture. One can do this by going backwards in time to a past which may be undocumented by writing. This is semantic anthropology, a linguistic approach which seeks to discover aspects of man's culture from his language. Cheikh Anta Diop was keenly interested in being able to speculate and predict on the basis of languages that he knew in the present. Ultimately one recognizes that resemblances between languages led to the appreciation of some relationship with those languages. The fact that Diop could use the Serer as an example to demonstrate its resemblance to something among the Peul suggests this. The rate at which languages change is variable. It appears that linguistic change is culture specific. Consequently, the social organization and political culture of a particular speech community can influence the speed at which languages change.

Based on the history of language change in Europe most linguists believe that the rate of change for all languages is both rapid and constant (Diagne, 1981:238). The idea that all languages change rapidly is not valid for all the world's languages. African languages change much slower than European languages (Armstrong, 1962). For example, African vocabulary items collected by Arab explorers over a thousand years ago are analogous to contemporary lexical items (Diagne, 1981:239). In addition there are striking resemblances between the ancient Egyptian language and Coptic, and Pharonic Egyptian and African languages (Diagne, 1981; Diop, 1977; Obenga, 1993).

The political stability of African political institutions has caused languages to change very slowly in Africa. Pawley and Ross (1993) argue that a sedentary life style may account for the conservative nature of a language. African oral traditions and the eye witness accounts of travelers to Africa, make it clear that African empires, although made up of diverse nationalities, illustrated continuity. To accommodate the plural nature of African empires, Africans developed a federal system of government (Niane, 1984). In fact, it is difficult to really describe ancient African state systems as empires, since this implies absolute rule or authority in a single imperial individual. This political state of affairs rarely existed in ancient Africa, because in each African community local leadership was elected by the people within the community. To have absolute power over several ethnic communities would have been impossible in most African political realities because of traditions, ancestors, rituals, ceremonies, and philosophies (Diop, 1987). For example the Egyptians often appointed administrators over the conquered territories from among the conquered people (Diop, 1981).

Now when we come to the continuity of many African languages we can see that this may result from the steady state nature of African political systems, and long standing cultural stability since neolithic times (Diop, 1981; Winters, 1985). This cultural stability has affected the speed at which African languages change. Ama Mazama, herself an Afrocentric linguistic scholar, with outstanding work in the area believes that it is essential to study linguistic connections between the continent and the Diaspora as well. One cannot stop with the rate of change on the continent, but must see that this type of method is applicable elsewhere. Her (1981:214) work suggests Diop's argument that "languages follow the migratory currents, the particular destinies of peoples, and fragmentation is the rule until an official effort, a political will, tries to expand a mode of expression to the detriment of others."

In Africa due to the relative stability of socio-political structures and settled life, there has not been enough pressure exerted on African societies as a whole and African speech communities in particular, to cause radical internal linguistic changes within most African languages. Permanent settlements led to a clearly defined system of inheritance and royal succession. These traits led to stability on both the social and political levels.

This leads to the hypothesis that linguistic continuity exist in Africa due to the stability of African socio-political structures and cultural systems. This relative cultural stability has led African languages to change more slowly than European and Asian languages. Diop (1974:153–154)) observed that, "First the evolution of languages, instead of moving everywhere at the same rate of speed seems linked to other factors; such as, the stability of social organizations or the opposite, social upheavals. Understandably in relatively stable societies man's language has changed less with the passage of time."

There is considerable evidence which supports the African continuity concept. Armstrong (1962) noted the linguistic continuity of African languages when he used glottochronology to test the rate of change in Yoruba. Comparing modern Yoruba words with a list of identical terms collected 130 years ago by Koelle, Armstrong found little if any internal or external changes in the terms. He (1962:285) concluded that:

> I would have said that on this evidence African languages are changing with glacial slowness, but it seems to me that in a century a glacier would have changed a lot more than that; perhaps it would be in order to say that these languages are changing with geological slowness.

Diop's theory of linguistic constancy recognizes the social role language plays in African language change. Language being a variable phenomenon has as much to do with a speaker's society as with the language itself. Thus social organization can influence the rate of change within languages. Meillet (1926:17) wrote that: "Since language is a social institution it follows that linguistics is a social science, and the only variable element to which one may appeal in order to account for a linguistic change is social change, of which language variations are but the consequences."

In the end it must be agreed that Diop has contributed much to African linguistics. He was a major proponent of the Dravidian-African relationship (Diop, 1974:116), and the African substratum in Indo-European languages in relationship to cacuminal sounds and terms for social organization and culture (1974:115). Diop (1978:113) also recognized that in relation to Arabic words, after the suppression of the first consonant, there is often an African root. Research in this area will have a profound impact on our understanding of the evolution of the Arabic culture. What is necessary to advance Diop's original thesis in this regards is a scholar sufficiently versed in Arabic and several African languages, particularly in the African Northeast and especially in the Sudan and Ethiopia region, to study this idea.

Diop's major linguistic effort has been the classification of Black African and Egyptian languages. Up until 1977 Diop's major linguistic concerns were morphological and phonological similarities between Egyptian and Black African languages. Diop (1977:77–84) explains many of his sound laws for the Egyptian-Black African connection. Even in saying this I am aware that this was only a small part of his linguistic interest. Diop was gifted as a creative thinker, indeed, as talented creatively as he was as a practical scientist. One cannot be a good scientist without being creative and Diop had a mind that was given to seeing connections, interrelationships, and metaphors. This is one source of his genius.

In *Parènte génétique de l'egyptien pharaonique et des langues négro africaines* (PGEPLNA), Diop (1974) explains in some detail his linguistic views in the introduction of this book. What he does by way of demonstrating to his readers the strong connections between the African languages is to show hundreds of cognate Wolof and Egyptian terms to support his thesis that there is a definite linguistic relationship between the languages of Black Africa and ancient Egypt which Diop sees as a Black African civilization. This relationship, he contends, does not only exist for Wolof, it is found in the connection with other African languages as well.

Diop enjoyed discoveries in correspondences of languages such as the following:

Egypt	Senegal
Atum	Atu
Sekmet	Sek
Keti	Keti
Kaba	Kaba
Antef	Anta
Perab	Fari
Meri	Meri
Saba	Sebe
Kare	Kare
Ba-Ra	Bara
Ramses	Rama
Bakari	Bakari

Nevertheless, Diop's major linguistic work, *Parentè gènètique de l'e-gyptien pharaonique et des langues negro-africaines,* remains the least read and perhaps the least understood of his scholarly works. This is because it is necessary to have command of several languages, including *Mdw Ntr,* the ancient Egyptian language in order to be able to engage the research thoroughly. Diop overcame linguistic barriers by studying many languages simultaneously. He was convinced that it was necessary to appreciate the structures and lexical varieties of languages to make progress on the interconnections of African cultures.

Another area of his concern was the linguistic connection between continental African languages and those of West Asia. Few scholars have taken him up on this thesis; however, Clyde Ahmad Winters has done more along these lines than any other African author. He has explored in depth the relationship between various continental languages and the Dravidian languages showing the similarity in the verbal, phonological, and lexical base of the languages. Using the techniques of semantic anthropology and linguistic Africology, Winters has been able to go backwards through what Diop called "the impenetrable past undocumented by written records."

It is probably true that language analysis alone allows one to use the contemporary artifact as a pathway to antiquity. This type of reconstruction is not easy, in fact, the reason it has not been taken up by many other writers is because it involves a level of skill in languages that is uncommon. It is not that you have to know African languages, you must also have some knowledge of the West Asian languages.

Diop (1974; 1977:xxix–xxxviv) is clear that the West Asians who were called Elamites and Sumerians were of Black origin. Following this line of thinking, Winters (1985, 1989, 1994) has spent considerable time advancing the idea that there is a clear linguistic affinity between African and West Asian languages. Part of the problem with the inquiry is that the people in the various regions of the world have been led to believe that such a connection is unthinkable, indeed, impossible to make. Again, Diop would lay this issue properly at the feet of the Western historians and anthropologists who were intent on demonstrating the isolation of the African people in order to more fully exercise hegemony over the world. What Diop did in raising this question, that is, the issue of an affinity between African and West Asian languages is to thrust Africa into a larger context. In reality, this had already been done by the facts on the ground since migration out of Africa to other continents was a known fact and a reality. We also know that the African people who left the continent did not leave empty handed; they left with conceptions, perceptions, attitudes, and the ability to use language.

It remains for a cadre of scholars to rise to the task that Diop, Mazama, and Winters has suggested as a valuable field of research. I would add that the research could and should come from both sides of the Indian or as we say, East African Ocean. There is no reason for Dravidian and Tamil scholars not to explore these depths themselves as a way of reclaiming their own past. Much of the research that was proposed by Diop can only be undertaken by joint teams of scholars. When this is a reality we will have understood how this great thinker conceived of a universe where all parts of the African world would be reconnected.

CHAPTER 4

THE AFROCENTRIC PARADIGM:
A FRAMEWORK FOR RE-VISIONING
AFRICAN HISTORY

Diop can be said to have been one of the first historians to articulate a decidedly Afrocentric point of view. He was clear in his belief that in order to write African history one had to allow Africans to write their own story. An Afrocentric view of African history is written from the standpoint of African people as subjects of human experiences. One of the cardinal truths in Afrocentricity is the fact that ancient Kemet was a Black African civilization. Like Diop, Afrocentrists claim a Black origin of Egypt and a Black influence on the civilizations of Europe. Some African American authors such as R. B. Lewis (1844), who wrote the book, *Light and Truth, collected from the Bible and the ancient and modern history, containing the universal history of the Colored and Indian Race from Creation of the World to the Present*; George W. Williams (1982), *History of the Negro Race in America from 1619 to 1880 . . . and an Historical Sketch of Africa*, and Rufus L. Perry (1893), *The Cushite or Descendants of Ham* used the ability they had to search for ways to vindicate Africans. Some of the arguments were based on the Bible, a principal source of authority for many of their readers. These pre-Diopian responses were a part of an attempt to elevate the status of Africans in world history through discovery of instances where the Black presence appeared in the Christian sacred text.

Cheikh Anta Diop was responsible for maintaining an African idea of history which included documents and archaeological records. It was important to understand that written records, eye-witness accounts, and evidence of products and materials produced were all a part of the story of Africa. Diop understood this and it added to the multidimensionality of his research. Diop knew of the work of Homer in much the same way as Du Bois (DuBois, 1946; Diop, 1974). Furthermore, he consulted the writings of Herodotus as Du Bois had done (DuBois, 1946:21; Diop, 1974) and also the work of Diodorus Siculus (DuBois, 1946:22; Diop, 1974). In his own writings Clyde Winters has confirmed that the "classicists were often biased, yet they report in clear prose the African role in the rise of civilization and culture in Africa and Asia and give internal credibility to their statements about African people."

DuBois, as Winter points out, outlined a world history on the Black races. In this book DuBois (1946:ix–xi) makes it clear that he admired the work of many of his contemporaries such as J. A. Rogers and Hansberry, authors who had began their quest to discover the African past after reading *The Negro*. As early as 1946, DuBois (1946:98–100; 176–194) argued that Africans founded civilizations in Egypt and Arabia. It was in this connection that he demonstrated that the Egyptians were the mothers and fathers of human civilization. This book, *The World and Africa*, must be read and re-read to see how Du Bois' work preceded Diop's and laid the foundation for the younger man's explosive thesis and proof that the ancient Egyptians were black-skinned. Thus, Diop would do as DuBois had done suggest that European capitalism, doctrine of White superiority and greed, fueled Europe's lies about African history and culture (DuBois, 1946:80).

One of the female scholars to take on the subject of the African origin of civilization was Drusilla D. Houston. She wrote an important work with the title, *Wonderful Ethiopians of the Ancient Cushite*

Empire. In this volume she argues that the civilizations of southern Arabia, Greece, India and Persia were founded by Africans from the Nile Valley.

William Leo Hansberry was born in 1894, and was the first historian to teach African studies at a major university in the world. Dr. Hansberry became interested in African history after reading DuBois' *The Negro*. This book led Hansberry to decide to learn more about Kush and ancient Ethiopia. In 1922, Hansberry went to Howard University in Washington, D.C., where he became the first American to teach courses on African history on a regular basis.

Carter G. Woodson is often called the "Father of African American History" because he devoted his life to the teaching of African American and African history. In books on Africa, Woodson discussed Africa and its cultural heritage in an effort to reeducate a public that had been miseducated. Woodson was the founding editor of the *Journal of Negro History*, which still publishes many articles on African history.

83

In a powerful book, Maghan Keita contends that the work of Diop is central to the introduction of a new, open, plural historiography. *Race and the Writing of History* marks Meghan Keita as an inheritor of the historiography set out by Diop. Of course, Keita demonstrates in this book that African American historians had sought to challenge the reigning orthodoxy on African history prior to Diop's intervention. Indeed, it is the work of the English scholar, Martin Bernal, that anticipates the theoretical work of Keita. Bernal's discussion of the Afro-Asiatic roots of Greek civilization allows Keita to examine the way African American historians had treated the subjects of ancient Egypt, Ethiopia, and the role those cultures played in making Greece.

Although Keita uses the so-called "cultural wars" of the 1990s as a starting point in his analysis of the role of the African American historians he is clearly writing about ancient history. His discussion focuses on race as a category, that is, a conceptual category and how it, has influenced the writing of history. Indeed, the idea of Black people writing history had been as foreign to some White scholars as the idea of Blacks making history. Keita demonstrates that both activities have been natural to the African American. He is particularly keen to show that Frank Snowden, Carter G. Woodson, William Leo Hansberry, and W. E. B. Du Bois understood much about the ancient world and could write Africa in the context of history without much effort. Of course, Snowden, of all these historians was the most intimidated by the hegemony of Europe over Africa. Nevertheless, the book advances the ideas of Diop and becomes in the process a Diopian project where the writer sees the importance of Theophile Obenga, Valentin Mudimbe, and Ali Mazrui in the struggle against the falsification and misinterpretation of African history, although it is easy for an Afrocentrist to see that Obenga, Mudimbe, and Mazrui have different projects.

Ama Mazama (2003), one of the key Afrocentric scholars of our times, has articulated the view that our destiny resides in the Diopian notion that we must retake the writing of our history as a part of the paradigm for overcoming the legacies of enslavement. Such a battle plan for African intellectuals must be executed with academic integrity, methodological soundness, and social responsibility. But Mazama is determined in her writings to see that we consider the emergence of the Afrocentric paradigm, in the Diopian sense, as one of the elements in our work.

Innocent Onyewuenyi's *The African Origin of Greek Philosophy: An Exercise in Afrocentrism* (1993) outlined how Western philosophers suppressed the role of Africa in philosophy. Europeans created myths about African history that allowed ignorance to reign in many communities. Indeed, Count Volney (1913:74–75) said "that prejudice is the only safeguard of that which cannot be defended in the open. What cannot be answered must be hushed up." Among the philosophers who were involved in suppression, according to Onyewuenyi, were Hegel, Lewes, Glenn, Fuller, and McInerny.

Few African intellectuals before Diop had developed such a keen awareness of history. Although he has grounded himself in the histories and historiography of Hegel, Fichte, Marx, and Engels, it was, perhaps, his family tradition in Senegal which had the greatest impact on his historical consciousness. The greatest writer in Africa in terms of production of work had been one of his great ancestors, Cheikh Amadou Bamba, Cheikh M'Backe's grandfather. Diop was aware as a young boy of the significant contribution to scholarship, although religious, of his family and he was also aware of the role they had played in the resistance to French occupation. These were important factors in the creation of his historical consciousness.

Now how did Diop use historical consciousness in his own work? He made history a companion to all of his inquiries. If he did essentially scientific work, say, the melanin content of a mummy, he would first establish the historical data related to the age of the mummy by determining its dynastic date and perhaps characterizing the particular dynasty. One of the best examples of what he thought of the uses of history appear in his book, *The Cultural Unity of Black Africa*, where he is writing of the role of the matriarchy in Africa. Showing the difference between the African concept of queen and that of Europe and Asia he uses an example of Queen Semiramis.

THE IDEA OF QUEENSHIP

According to the legend of Queen Semiramis, which is reported by Diodorus Siculus, she was the daughter of Venus and a Syrian shepherd. She was raised by doves that had nested in the spot where she was abandoned. Shepherds discovered the child and gave it to the head of the royal sheep-folds whose name was Simma, hence the

name Semiramis. When she was of age she was given in marriage
to Menones, one of the king's courtiers, who took her to live in
Nineveh where she had two children, Hyapate and Hydaspe.

One day King Ninus went to battle against Bactria. He took with
him Menones and his wife as part of the king's entourage. As the
battle raged, Ninus was repulsed by the Bactrians. Semiramis, used
her brain to devise a scheme that diverted the attention of the Bactrians while the soldiers were able to skirt the fortifications of the
town. When it was known that the scheme had been devised by
Semiramis she was brought to the king who asked for her hand in
marriage, proposing to her husband that he give her up to him. The
king threatened to blind Menones, but he hanged himself, and Semiramis became queen. She had a son, Ninyas, for the king. Finally
when King Ninus died, he left Semiramis as queen. She is credited
with the founding or the improvement of the city of Babylon.

I have paraphrased this story of Diodorus' retold by Diop. How
this is seen by Diop gives us an indication of what he thought of the
concept of queenship among the people of Asia. He cautions that
this is a legendary tale and should not be taken literally. However, it
is a fact that Semiramis existed and by studying such a legend it is
possible to gather some insight into the sociology and temperament
of the people who produced the legend. Nevertheless, Diop writes,
"it would be necessary to know at what period the legend was born,
if it is indeed characteristic of the historical period of which it is
wished to attribute it. These ideal conditions being impossible to
fulfill, there must always remain a large part which has merely been
interpreted, which it is possible, at best, to attempt to restrict. But
it is very necessary to proceed thus, if one wishes to try writing the
history of these early periods of humanity of which very little evidence survived (Diop, 1989:126). So we see Diop's method.

As an intellectual he is aware of the conditions for history, the
nature of historical evidence, and the possibility of interpretation.

This is the work of science. But now let us take a look at how Diop explains the Semiramis story in relationship to African matriarchy. He says, "Semiramis was not, like the African queens, a princess by birth, sanctified as queen by tradition. She was a courtesan of humble birth, who was led to take power by favorable circumstances. She was thus an adventuress, like all the Asian queens. Behind them there was no matriarchal tradition (Diop, 1989:126–127).

Here we already have one of Diop's central beliefs about history and that is the historical record must be interpreted. His life's work, of course, demonstrated that you cannot interpret history without some background studies in other fields. This is why as an intellectual he devoted his time to sociology, anthropology, linguistics, physics, and any other science or study that would allow him a broad rendering of information and knowledge about a certain historical fact.

A PROPER READING OF WORLD HISTORY

87

I have not gotten the idea that Diop believed in some ultimate or universal reading of world history under the watchful eye of a Creator. Nor is he to be read in the more mysterious and spookish way that the universe itself can have a purpose and thus we are all parts of that purpose. In effect, if we are unable to grasp the thing within our own consciousness, then the thing does not exist which is the same thing as saying the existence does not matter. Who can know if the universe has a purpose, that is, who can grasp this mentally and explain it without knowing fully the universe? To know such is to be the Creator. There is nothing in Cheikh Anta Diop that speaks to this type of reasoning in history. I think that he understood history in the sense that any reflection on the African past or the human past should allow us to discern the direction history is moving. Of course, any proper discernment of that direction is based on an adequate reading of the past. If we misread the records from the past, we will not be able to read correctly the movement toward the future. Thus, the history of Africa is none other than the progress of humanity from tradition to generation to tradition. This is Diop's view.

One of the main factors which separates Diop's line of thinking from that of Hegel, the leading European thinker, is that Diop includes Africa and its civilizations in the chronology of world history. This may not seem to be a significant difference to the casual reader but to the African person, lay or scholar, the omission of Africa from the chronology of world history by a major European thinker is itself representative of the racist nature of the Western history. Hegel, for example, begins his account of history with what he terms "the Oriental World." He means by this Persia, India, and China. Of course, as far as Hegel is concerned China and India were stationary, not progressive societies. They had reached a certain point but had not continued to advance. These civilizations, like Africa, were "outside the history of the world" because they had not participated in the overall process of world development. This was the basis of his philosophy of history. He believed that true history started with the Persian Empire because it was the first empire to come into existence and then to pass away. But this is bad history in the sense that it allows Hegel to neglect the entire continent of Africa. Egypt, the world's first nation, indeed, the first country to bring together disparate groups, forty-two altogether, into one nation, is missing from Hegel's account of world history (Breasted, 1962).

What are we to make of such omission? How can we rationalize this ignorance on the part of the most famous European thinker with the possible exception of Plato? I do not think it can be done; rationality escapes this situation. This is what Diop saw in the thinking of writers like Hegel. The questions one might put are these, are these deliberate omissions or are they the results of authentic ignorance about the African continent? Diop comes down on the side of deliberate falsification because the only way that the German Hegel could uphold the Aryan thesis was to dismiss from history the cases that challenged his logic. It seemed that the reasoning was that if you ignore Egypt and Nubia, for example, they may go away. Fortunately we now see this for what it was and the corrective has already been put into place by the consummate intellectual as well as those who preceded him with refutations of Hegel's view.

There is nothing in Diop that speaks of unfreedom or authoritarianism. As an intellectual he was willing to take on all comers. His reaction to his opponents was to debate the arguments or to write responses to their commentaries. This kept him rather busy. He knew that those who challenged his major theses had to be confronted and their arguments engaged. He enjoyed debate and polemics and there were few who could stand with him in debate. When the progressive students of Dakar met with him to discuss Marxism, political economy, race, philosophy, or worker's right he would invite them to contest his ideas just to sharpen his own mind.

Asa Hilliard (2002) responding to the criticism of the American classicist Mary Lefkowitz takes issue with her characterization of Diop as "Senegal's humanist and scientist" without giving further information about his credentials. Hilliard (2002: 61) writes "Dr. Diop earned his Ph.D. in Egyptology from the University of Paris, Sorbonne. In the course of his higher education, he had formal study and practical experience with the great physicists and chemists of Europe, himself directing the radiocarbon dating laboratory in Dakar, Senegal." What Hilliard seeks to do is demonstrate how callous the opponents of Diop have been in trying to discredit his work. Instead of engaging his theses some writers often attempt to diminish his intellectual credibility. Thus, to speak of the intellectual as a "humanist and scientist" and placing "humanist" in the first place is a rhetorical act. Hilliard (2002:63) is aware of this endeavor to diminish Diop and so he continues, "Dr. Diop was highly trained in anthropology, including physical anthropology, and was even a linguist of note. Further, he was a historian and had an unusually developed grasp of political economy. He was uniquely qualified to integrate a variety of relevant academic disciplines. His intimate knowledge of continental African culture as well as his intimate knowledge of European continental culture, including the ancient past of both, makes him an unparallel expert in the study of Kemet and Greece."

BATTLING THE CULTURE OF DISBELIEF

All historical events have both a social and a political role. Cheikh Anta Diop understood that all human actions helped to create history. It was not something outside of Africans but deeply inside of African experiences. Ultimately when we speak of historical events in a temporal sense or historical evidences in a sense of historiography we are talking about humanity and consciousness. What Diop sought to do was to help reconstruct a usable past for the African world. This is not to say that the past as it had been interpreted by Europeans was not usable; only to say that it was usable for Europeans. What Africa needed was a past based on our understanding of our own experiences not interpreted through the eyes of those who were bent on sustaining conquest. One of the great contest between the Black and White races has been over who will interpret the history of Africa. This should not come as a surprise since African history is the earliest history of humans and civilization.

In Diop's mind, history provided us with an appreciation of how humans have acted in the past thus giving us current lessons for how we might act in similar situations in the present or future. It also was a way to see where we are situated in the great flow of human history and thus what may confront us in the future. Therefore, in his mind, history was about the past and the future. Quite frankly, not even reason itself was any stronger in the interpretation of the past than history.

Diop was a reasonable historian, an eminently brilliant interpreter of the past, using all the avenues logical evidences afforded. But to understand Diop you must see that he was a political man and his politics was in the interests of the future of Africa. When he is thinking about the future he is thinking about how to inspire the youth to reach the highest heights. To do this it is important to have a usable and a meaningful history that has been constructed from the actual facts of human living.

One must contrast Cheikh Anta Diop with Frank M. Snowden, Jr., often called by White historians one of the best Black students of antiquity. Snowden entered the world of antiquity with impressive credentials in the Western world. He received his Ph.D. from Harvard in classics, became the chairman of the Department of Classics at Howard University, and authored several books, including his magnum opus, *Blacks in Antiquity: Ethiopians in the Greco-Roman Experience.* Unquestionably Snowden was the most highly trained classicist in the African American community during his time and no classicist since George G. M. James had commanded as much attention. Although James' audience was mainly African and Snowden's mainly White, the work produced by both men created a discussion in the United States that greatly enhanced the discourse on antiquity.

Of course, as I have indicated, Diop was interested in a usable past for Africans. No such formality interested Frank Snowden whose ambition was to present what he claimed to be an objective account of Blacks in antiquity. It disturbed him that many African scholars had abandoned what he considered to be the best principles of Western scholarship in search for political advancement or the use of history as politics. The intellectual condition of Snowden raises an important point about the practice of science. There have always been in the African community two types of African scholars: (1) those committed to a liberation *praxis*, and (2) those committed to careerism. While this may seem to be a limiting bifurcation, it is a truism that some African scholars are concerned with the purpose and objective of their work while others are concerned with how they will advance as individuals within the structures of the Western world. Clearly Snowden was of the latter type and Diop was of the first type. Both types have contributed greatly to our understanding of the past but the more consciously committed scholars have been those who have helped to save us from mental oppression and have rescued us from the damage of Western imperial thought. Unfortunately, one cannot say this of Snowden.

Snowden's failures are Diop's successes in historiography. They start from different places in their minds. Consider Snowden's (1979:vii) opening paragraph in the preface to Blacks in Antiquity:

> Among the many peoples who entered the Greco-Roman world were the dark and black-skinned Ethiopians of Africa. The experiences of these Africans who reached the alien shores of Greece and Italy constituted an important chapter in the history of classical antiquity. An examination of the resultant intermingling of these peoples enables us to study an early encounter of White Europeans with dark and black Africans.

Snowden introduces us to his problem in an un-self conscious way. He is seeing the issue of Africans in antiquity as if he is a White person, that is, he is writing from the standpoint of Africans as the others. The most revealing aspect of this problem is in the title of the book itself, Blacks in Antiquity, as if that constitutes an issue. The issue is "Whites in Antiquity", but again that is another problem of his historiography. The immediate issue is that Snowden considers Blacks, by which he means, Africans, as interlopers in antiquity which, in effect, *belongs* to Europeans, specifically Greeks and Romans. This is where his training in the Greek and Roman classics betrays his intellect. Snowden's title "Blacks in Antiquity" is about how Africans people were seen by Greeks and Romans. To create such a title and to pursue such research as he has done, quite frankly, in a spectacular fashion is to add to the Western perception that the Greeks and Romans were more ancient than Africans. His idea is to discover how the Greeks and Romans *saw* Africans rather than how Africans *saw* Greeks and Romans.

Thus, it was easy for him to write "among the peoples to enter the Greco-Roman world were the dark and black-skinned Ethiopians" because he does not consider the fact, at least, here that the Ethiopians predated the Greeks and Romans and if anything a more intelligent discussion would have been how the Greeks and Romans entered the Ethiopian-Nubian-Kemetic world. What we find in Snowden is important information that constitutes a thorough appreciation of how Greeks and Romans viewed Africans but the orientation of the research, the aim of his project, and the objective of his arguments are to prove that Blacks existed in the classical Greek and Roman world. I am convinced that his intentions were good and may have come from the vindicationist perspective of African scholarship where the author is trying to "prove" that Black people did this or that, but it was wrong-headed and instead of advancing Africa Snowden's work simply served to show that the Greeks and Romans knew Black people.

In stark contrast, the work of Cheikh Anta Diop demonstrated that Greek and Roman civilization existed on the foundations that had been laid by classical African civilizations. In this regard, Diop is more in line with George G. M. James who argued in *Stolen Legacy* that there was no Greek philosophy only stolen African philosophy. Both Diop and James understood that Kemet predated Greece by several thousand years and that if one wanted to look for antiquity it would be more profitable to look in the direction of Africa rather than Europe. Cheikh Anta Diop was convinced by his experiences

93

that Europe and White scholars would never adequately prepare Africans to research their own past; Snowden was an example of that failure. It could have been Diop's own fate as a student of France's top university, La Sorbonne, but like so many Black scholars, including W. E. B. Du Bois, Carter G. Woodson, John Hope Franklin, and others, it was necessary to sort out the weeds from the useful grain in the training one received from the White institutions. In some of those institutions the teachers and professors were White racist whose ambition was to advance European concepts of superiority. Perhaps it was Diop's practical bent that caused him to question many of the theoretical and analytical positions of his teachers.

It is easy to forget that Cheikh Anta Diop was a politician, though not as successful in a practical sense as many of his compatriots. But he appreciated the fact that history would judge his actions and that a people could find a guide to their conduct through history, but politics and the political objective were not his fundamental concern. Diop was more interested in discovering in every possible corner of the earth the proper historical record of Africa because he felt that it had been so badly distorted by the Europeans that it would mean African people would forever be questioning their own ancestors based on a false record. This is why he raised the issue of the falsification of history. It was a fabrication, something made up, comprised of the pieces that fit into the European's own puzzle but had limited edition in the African story. This is the context of Diop's historical imagination.

In defense of Africa, Diop never pushes a triumphalist or romanticized approach to the history of the continent. Such an approach would serve to raise consciousness by avoiding the discussion of contrary points of view. Perhaps better than anyone I have read Diop is skilled at presenting the opposing views, that is, those views that are contrary to his and then pointing out where he differs with those who have been considered experts. Mythmaking is not a part of his intention. While making myths certainly has had its role in the historical imagination, the idea of learning from the past or discovering and reconstructing a usable past has a lot more to do removing the cataracts from the public's eye. Diop seeks to open the vision of the public, to view the varieties of African history and culture from the standpoint of the African. This is the power of his evidences.

The power of what Diop did was to cripple the ruling myths of the Western world's historiography. Of course, all forms of history are selective and one may argue that the Western myths are no more misleading than those of Africa or Asia. This may be right on the surface but only the Western myths seek to isolate the world for itself. In doing this, the West pushes other cultures and civilizations to the margins of history. Diop returns Africa to its centered place in the history of human civilization and he returns Black people to the history of Egypt.

Thus, one of the main actions of the historian must be to question the dominant mythologies and to provide alternative ways of looking at the past. What Cheikh Anta Diop accomplished in his works was a way to destabilize the Eurocentric construction of the ancient world and to open up the possibility of another way of seeing. This is Diop's radical contribution to the study of human history.

Recognizing the disbelief that appeared in the European mind about the Blackness of the ancient Egyptians Diop found it necessary to rely on all forms of research. However, as he (1974:1) notes in *African Origin of Civilization*, "eyewitnesses of that period formally affirm that the Egyptians were blacks." Of course, Diop was not finished with his argument simply because he made a statement, he further identified those whose accounts he took as fact. Thus, Herodotus, the 5th century B.C. historian, says that the Egyptians he saw were Black. To prove that the flooding of the Nile cannot be caused by melting snow, Herodotus cites as one reason the observation that "the natives of the country are black with heat . . ." (Ibid.). This is still not enough to convince the naysayers, so Diop calls upon the testimony of Ethiopians as produced by a Greek writer of the 1st century B.C. The Egyptians are a colony of the Ethiopians according to Diodorus Siculus (1738, Book 3:341):

> The Ethiopians say that the Egyptians are one of their colonies which was brought into Egypt by Osiris. They even allege that this country was originally under water, but that the Nile, dragging much mud as it flowed from Ethiopia, had finally filled it in and made it a part of the continent . . . They add that from them, as from their authors and ancestors, the Egyptians get most of their laws. It is from them that the Egyptians have learned to honor kings as gods and bury them with such pomp; sculpture and writing were invented by the Ethiopians. The Ethiopians cite evidence that they are more ancient than the Egyptians, but it is useless to report that here).

Another contribution that we have touched upon is Diop's use of a multiplicity of evidences. Human beings have left a great variety of things, objects, tools, that the historian can use to demonstrate evidence. It is not something that is limited to words on a page. This is what our best scholars have understood over the years. They knew that oral narratives, music, symbolism, carvings, and dance are as much a part of evidence as documentary information. There is no question that Diop was better at collecting an array of evidences than any other African scholar before him. This is where all of his study and reflection entered the service of the African world. Although there remained Whites who did not want to believe the evidence presented by Diop, he was undeterred by the naysayers. His task was to reconstruct the history of ancient Africa. Thus, disbelief was the Eurocentric defense against this powerful movement.

Basil Davidson once told me that there was an attitude of "disbelief" that comes over Europeans when they confront African intelligence and industry. It was, he said, an attitude that was rooted in the belief in the superiority of the White race. In one sense it may be that Egypt's own turbulent history has created the confusion in some people's minds, but I dare say that the scholars know the truth. Diop contends that the series of conquests of Egypt might have caused the interpretation of its past to be one of great complication. He (Diop, 1974:10) writes that "When Herodotus visited it, Egypt had already lost its independence a century earlier. Conquered by the Persians in 525 B.C., from then on it was continually dominated by the foreigner: after the Persians came the Macedonians under Alexander (333 B.C.), the Romans under Julius Caesar (50 B.C.), the Arabs in the seventh century, the Turks in the sixteenth century, the French with Napoleon, then the English at the end of the nineteenth century."

Perhaps it was Hegel who most corrupted the European's intellectual tradition with the falsification of African history. He is not alone by any measure, but as the most significant European scholar in modern history his arguments against Africa and for the triumphalism of Europe have become pervasive in the thinking of the West.

In his *Lectures on the History of Philosophy*, Hegel (1974:21–22) claims that "the only distinction between the Africans and the Asiatics on the one hand, and the Greeks, Romans, and moderns on the other, is that the latter know and it is explicit for them, that they are free, but the others are so without knowing that they are, and thus without existing as being free" (pp. 21–22). Not only is this statement blatantly false; it is clearly filled with Eurocentric superiority. However, he (Ibid: 63) he also states that "it is a legend universally believed, that Pythagoras, for instance, received his philosophy from India and Egypt; the fame of the wisdom of these people, which wisdom is understood also to contain philosophy, is an old one." The question is why should it have been "an old" legend if there were no truth to it. On what is it based? Why would Pythagoras go to Egypt in the first place? Why not find the source of his philosophy in Europe?

Hegel's ethnocentrism is rarely criticized by European writers, many of whom have literally accepted his racism as a part of their own perspective of the world. When Hegel (Ibid:66) asks "but is the admiration of God as revealed in natural things as such, in trees and animals as opposed to what is human, far removed from the religion of the ancient Egyptians which derived its knowledge of what is divine from the ibis, or from cats and dogs"? Hegel has set up a hierarchical division that suggests Europe's response to the divine is based on something different than that of Africa. But he misunderstood the nature of the divine in ancient Egypt and Africa. No Egyptian saw religion as emanating from animals.

Yet Hegel obviously knew or suspected that the Greeks had been influenced by Africans. He (Ibid:150) writes that "They (the Greeks) certainly received the substantial beginnings of their religion, culture, their common bonds of fellowship, more or less from Asia, Syria and Egypt; but they have so greatly obliterated the foreign nature of this origin, and it is so much changed, worked upon, turned round, and altogether made so different, that what they, as we, prize, know, and love in it, is essentially their own." This is self-congratulatory rhetoric. Indeed, Hegel is correct to note that the beginnings of the Greek culture must be found elsewhere. Bernal has shown persuasively that those origins are in Africa and Asia. Hegel recognized this evidence but sought to dismiss it by saying that it had been so changed, modified, and worked upon, that it was now essentially only the work of the Greeks (Bernal, 1987:317–320).

Furthermore, Hegel (Ibid:172) gives the European credit for things that are questionable. He says of Thales, the first Greek philosopher that

> voyages to Phoenicia are recorded of him, which however, rest on
> vague tradition; but that he was in Egypt in his old age seems
> undoubted. It was to the effect that Thales taught the Egyptians to

measure the height of their pyramids by shadow—by taking the relation born by the height of a man to his shadow. If this were something new to the Egyptians, they must have been very far back in the theory of geometry.

This is the kind of half truth that has dominated much of the European writing about Egyptian influence on the Greeks. Hegel (Ibid:197), with an appreciation for Pythagoras' achievements writes, "as Pythagoras traveled with a scientific purpose, it is said that he had himself initiated into nearly all the mysteries of Greeks and of Barbarains, and thus he obtained admission into the order or caste of the Egyptian priesthood."

One of the continuing falsifications in the Western academy and in the popular imagination is that of the color of the ancient Egyptians. Although Diop settled this issue years ago with his book, *The African Origin of Civilization*, there remain White writers and some Blacks who have never examined Diop's work or if they have, simply avoid dealing with it. They do not know that the debate is and therefore gives inane and insincere defenses of the indefensible. Thus, Diop's thesis that the ancient Egyptians were black-skinned has come under assault by pseudo-scientific White nationalist thinkers such as John Tiffany (2004). In a piece entitled "The Racial Makeup of the Original Egyptians", we discover all of the racist possibilities in one article. As is the case in the most scurrilous replies to Afrocentricity, Tiffany's article lacks authority as an intellectual argument because of his venom announced as an argument. He mentions Cheikh Anta Diop and Theophile Obenga in a gratuitous manner, puts forth the rehashed arguments of Eurocentrists who do not understand the depth of their own ignorance, and condemns those who express historically factual information.

There are many problems with Tiffany's position but it is typical of the many assaults that have been made by Whites on ancient

African history. First, he criticizes Afrocentricity without defining it but spews forth pejorative statements such as "Afrocentrism is a kind of pseudo-history that was concocted by those who felt that White and Asian people seemed to play too large a role in historiography" (Tiffany, 2004:6). This statement is untrue and nothing more than a ruse. That fact that Tiffany does not provide a definition given by Afrocentrists of Afrocentricity and does not state where Diop or any Afrocentrists ever made the claims he attributes to them means that he has essentially constructed a "straw" argument and he is the one who has "concocted" something. His statement is therefore presented as a decoy and any victory in his mind is a hollow one at that.

Diopian historiography is based on the fact that African people are central to their own story and that no one can tell the African story better than African people. Diop understood that Europeans will always try to tell our story from their own point of view and it will never be a story based on the facts of our lives. Their interpretations are always in support of White hegemony as seen in the case of John Tiffany. Diop presents his historiography as a critical inquiry into the place or location of African within the context of history. In relationship to Egypt or any other African culture the Afrocentrists seek to interrogate the role of Africans in their own history. It is not pseudo-history; it is the presentation of the African story within the context of the centrality of Africans in their own story. It is, in a way, more than history; it is an orientation to history. It is a critique, by virtue of its centering idea, of the falsification of facts.

To challenge Cheikh Anta Diop's construction of history one must meet him on equal grounds: truth, investigation, knowledge, and expertise. Tiffany's article reveals that he is devoid of these qualities and thus he is no match for the Imhotepian scholarship of Diop. Moreover, his work lacks ethical content, the foundation of Diop's search for truth about Africa after such a long rule of the

Eurocentric racist historiography. Diop dissects the falsehoods and fake information submitted by Eurocentrists. When Tiffany writes that "the Afrocentrists decry true history as Eurocentric" he is assuming a centrality for Europe that does not exist either chronologically or philosophically in the ancient world. Eurocentric history cannot be equated with true history (Tiffany, 2004:8). This is not only false it is arrogant. In fact, history is history.

Tiffany develops both theoretical and data problems with his construction against Diop's thesis. For example, in trying to fashion an argument against Afrocentric orientations to data or Afrocentric approaches to the historical record Tiffany lays two arguments at the feet of contemporary scholars. One has to do with the Blackness of the ancient Egyptians and the second has to do with the question of melanin. This second issue is a diversion that was never dealt with by Diop except in a scientific way when he measured the amount of melanin in the mummies. Of course, others have taken the discussion of this widely distributed pigment to other levels not intended by Diop. Thus, it is misleading to lay at Diop's feet or those of the Afrocentrists the charge that they believe in some mystical power of melanin for Black people. Tiffany does this to divert attention from the weakness of his argument against the Blackness of the ancient Egyptians. Diop was not a melanin scholar. Trying to tag him or Afrocentrists with some "wild eyed" notions of melanin is meant to discredit the main thesis: the ancient Egyptians were Black people.

Tiffany's arguments are downhill from this point. He argues in an odd way without context, evidence, or documentation. For example, he (2004:5) writes a summary of what he calls "the bizarre cosmogonic doctrine of Afrocentrism." He (Ibid.) declares that the Afrocentrists claim that "when, in accordance with the will of Allah, the Earth was separated from Luna by an explosion in the year 65,999,999,998,062 B.C., there appeared on the planet the black race." Of course, Tiffany does not provide a source for this supposedly "Afrocentric" summary of the origin of the Black race. This is the most bizarre of arguments against Afrocentricity and Diopian historiography because it has nothing to do with the thesis advanced by Diop nor those advanced by Afrocentrists. No Afrocentrists has ever made a claim such as the one that Tiffany sets up and then destroys.

Obviously Tiffany has never read *Civilization or Barbarism: An Authentic Anthropology* by Cheikh Anta Diop. Had he read the book prior to his essay in the *Barnes Review* and he may have refrained from ignorant statements. In the first chapter, Diop deals with Prehistory, Race and History: Origin of Humanity and Racial Differentiation. What does he cite to begin his discussion? He (Diop, 1981:11) cites the research of Dr. Louis Leakey who placed the birthplace of humanity in the Great Lakes region of East Africa around the Omo Valley. There is nothing hocus pocus about this fact. Humankind followed the principle of Gloger Law which calls for warm-blooded animals to be pigmented in hot and humid climates, thus the first humans, originating near the Equator, were heavily pigmented and black. All the other races, including Tiffany's race, derived from the Black race by direct filiation as all other continents were populated from Africa.

Diop cites the historical, anthropological, archaeological records. Now we are able to cite even the biological records through studies of mitachondrial DNA. The oldest records of hominids go back to about 6 million years and the earliest records of *homo sapiens sapiens* extend back to about 300,000 years ago. Thus, Tiffany's bizarre statements have no basis in fact when arguing against Diop or the Afrocentrists. As usual he gives neither references nor documentation for the statements attributed to Afrocentrists in an effort to avoid serious scrutiny of the statements. The aim is to deflect the power of the Afrocentric critique of Eurocentrists and to minimize the importance of Diop's claim that the ancient Egyptians were black skinned people.

Of course, it is on one hand irrational for Europeans to be arguing to claim an African civilization as their own, but on the other it is a part of the strategy of "cutting the heart" out of Africa in order to claim that it has no ancient civilization. Egypt puts a lie to that claim. It is interesting that Africans do not claim Europe or Asia. Indeed, the Asians do not claim Africa or Europe, It is only the Europeans who seek to claim a civilization clearly out of their cultural sphere. There is evidence neither in history nor in anthropology that claims the ancient Egyptians had white skin and straight hair. There is ample evidence stating that the ancient Egyptians had black skin and wooly hair. Herodotus, Diodorus, and Aristotle all attest to the Blackness of the ancient Egyptians.

Tiffany's argument is a diatribe against the thorough scholarship of Diop and is an attack that is remarkable for its vile. He (Ibid: 6) writes "The Afrocentric scholars such as Theophile Obenga and Cheikh Anta Diop seek to sell books to individuals, including demoralized White liberals. . . ." In the first place, Professor Diop became an ancestor in 1986, eighteen years before Tiffany's article, which is an indication that the man is simply parading as a scholar. Had he known that Diop was dead he would not have made a statement saying he was trying to sell his books. Neither Diop nor Obenga can be called gross capitalists or entrepreneurs seeking profit instead of truth. I do not have time nor interest in pursuing the political or economic origin of Tiffany's position but he writes in a White nationalist magazine that masquerades as an intellectual journal. Obenga is trained in at least eight languages including Mbochi, Lingala, French, English, Latin, Egyptian, Coptic and Greek. His work speaks for him. Diop was a scholar with the same breadth of knowledge and erudition. Both have few peers. The fact that Tiffany reacts so emotionally to the findings of their research and scholarship only reveals the extreme emotional disorientation and intellectual blindness his own Eurocentric nativism induces in him.

If one is to attack Diop's position on the ancient Egyptians it is necessary to know the facts and to argue from evidence. Tiffany does neither. So many errors appear in his article that one would almost have to make a line by line refutation of points in order to bring sense to the issue. Let me point out the most egregious problems. Tiffany (Ibid) claims that "most Egyptologists would argue that the ancient Egyptians were an ethnic group of the Caucasian race" (p. 6). He cites no evidence that most Egyptologists would make such a claim. A declarative statement, no matter how strongly made, is not evidence. Furthermore, if such Egyptologists made such a claim it would be false, if by Caucasian they mean White or European or persons with straight hair and white or pale skin. In fact, the statement demonstrates not science but ignorance.

Egypt is on the African continent. Africa is a Black continent except for the invaders and the children of invaders who came into the continent. The farther back in time you go the blacker the continent is and the blacker is the land of Egypt. Egypt is neither in Asia nor in Europe. So where are the Caucasians that Tiffany imagine in Africa? Who are the Egyptologists who will not come out of the closet to defend this untenable position that the ancient Egyptians were Caucasians? Why is it that Tiffany will not give their names, quotes from their research, reports from the field, or other documentation? The reason for this lack of evidence is because no respectable Egyptologists, even the most racists, would be careless enough now to make such an inane statement.

Cheikh Anta Diop understood that ancient Egypt was Kemet, the land of the Blacks or the Black nation. Tiffany wants to claim that the term *Kmt* means black dirt. This is one more stratagem that has been used by Whites to claim Egypt for Europe. The ancient people of the land did not call their land Egypt, which is a Greek name, but Kemet. Now the meaning of Kemet is not debatable among Afrocentric scholars who read the ancient language. They are clear that the ancient Africans meant to claim the land as the Land of Black People or the Black Country. They had traveled to other parts of the world and seen many types of people. In Turkey or Greece they had seen White people, but in their own land, Kemet, it was the land of Black People. The word carries a piece of charcoal to represent Blackness and it carries a determinative which means city, country, or organized entity. Even if they were trying to say "black dirt" they would have used a different determinative, perhaps one that came from agriculture or irrigation. Thus, what we are witnessing in the attacks on Diop, Obenga, and the Afrocentrists is the fact that Europe has dominated the intellectual discourse on Africa, even ancient Africa, in the interest of racism and White hegemony for so long and without challenge, that now Eurocentrists do everything within their power to hold onto the falsehoods built up over many years. This leads to weird positions and explanations.

Tiffany (Ibid: 6) admits that "blacks have been present in Egypt from very early times" but seeks to deny that Egypt was originally Black. The issue is not the presence of Blacks in Egypt but when did those Blacks become Whites or when did other non-Blacks enter the land. That is the real issue. If there were non-Whites entering the land with the invasions of the Assyrians, Persians, Greeks, and Romans, then that is something to talk about. Arab presence in large numbers is traced to General El As's troops coming to the aid of Blacks in Egypt who wanted to throw off the yoke of Rome. This was 639–641 A.D. I once had a student in a large lecture class on Africa to ask me the question, "Why is the majority of Egyptians my complexion if it was a black civilization"? She looked like any other White student. I would not have mistaken her for a Black student or an Asian student. Her look was quite European. I said to her, "if you would not be too sensitive to tell us your ethnic background, would you tell us what is the origin of your parents"? She replied quite proudly, "My mother is Greek and my father is Arab." I said to her, "There you have it. Most people in Egypt are the descendants of mixed populations of Greeks, English, Arabs, Turks, and the native Egyptians, now called Nubians." She understood immediately. I pressed the point, "Go to Aswan and Abu Simbel and you will see the black people in the land right now." "Yes, I have seen them", she replied.

I think that one of the greatest obstacles to real progress and understanding of the Diopian historiography and historical information is the re-circulating of arguments that have been smashed by science time and time again. Thus, Tiffany cites the racist Earnest Sevier Cox from his 1923 book, *White America*, reprinted in 1966, saying that skeletal remains from Egypt showed that less than two percent of the remains showed that the ancient Egyptians were Black. Perhaps an additional two percent showed suspicion of "Negro blood." In 1923 it was totally impossible to determine the DNA of human remains. More important to me is the fact that Cox is quoted as saying "the hair in almost all cases presented no resemblance of Negro hair" (Ibid: 6). The problem with this statement is that it is not verifiable. What is verifiable are the examples of "black hair" found in the Cairo Museum. What is verifiable are the African braids found on the female mummies in the special mummy room at the Cairo museum. This is concrete evidence of the type of hair one finds in ancient Egypt. Of course, Tiffany seeks to confuse the readers with pictures of Greeks who occupied Egypt. Presenting Ptolemaic rulers as if they were the Egyptians who built the great temples and pyramids is a way to "steal" Egyptian history.

Another approach to appropriating African history is to put into print the most horrific lies. For example, Tiffany (2004:6) argues that from the 18th to 25th dynasty, the six centuries of great majestic achievement from Ahmose to Piankhy, "mark the decay of Egyptian civilization." He grabs the heart of the Egyptian culture and says, it means nothing. In fact, this is a blatant assault on the period of the Thutmoses III, Rameses II, Hatshepsut, Akhenaten, Tarharka, and Shabataka.

What astonishes me even after years of answering the reactionary commentaries of White writers is the pain of Eurocentric demise. Indeed, Tiffany tries to convince his readers, contrary to all evidence, that the ancient Egyptians were White and that it was impossible for Blacks to build the great civilization of Egypt. There must be a name for such intellectual sickness. Tiffany writes that "this Negroid monarchy was the result of intermixture with a ruling class that was originally white" (Ibid:6). How such nonsense can get published as argument is an indication that the small minds that seek to counter the scholarship of Cheikh Anta Diop are out of their depths. Clearly, Tiffany is not only inaccurate; he is irrational. If it is a "Negroid monarchy" then it is not the result of some "intermixture" with a White ruling class. Either it is a "Negroid monarchy" or it is not but Tiffany wants to have it both ways because he knows that the ancient monarchies of Egypt were Black. One asks, "what happened to the white ruling class if the ruling class is now black"? Where do we find this white ruling class in Africa? When did it appear in the Nile Valley?

To get around the fact that the Egyptians portrayed Africans kings of the earlier dynasties as Black, Tiffany contends that representations of Kings "created outside their own time cannot be relied upon as being accurate representations" (Ibid.). This is clearly an attempt at subterfuge. This would mean that a representation of George Washington as White is not necessarily an accurate representation. It would mean that the representation of Shaka, King of the Zulu, as Black would not necessarily be an accurate representation. We know about the accuracy of racial representation based on historical evidence. There has never been a reasoned argument to say Menes, the first king of the first dynasty, was White, European, Caucasian, Asian, Arab, or anything other than Black. There is no abnormality in the literature about the origins of the ancient Egyptians; racism alone is the generator of the wild theory of a White ancient Egypt.

Diop understood that it was perhaps the greatest mark of psychological and historical insecurity when a people seek to steal another's heroes and to claim them as their own. Listen to Tiffany's rationalizations about Akhenaten. He claims Akhenaten's "flattened nose" was caused by bandages (p. 7). Furthermore, Tiffany sees in Tuthmoses III a "Caucasian" because of his aquiline nose. This is a trivial, provincial and irrational notion based on some White or Eurocentric idea of what a Black person should look like. There is no one "look" for Black people. Tiffany is not finished with his attempt to "steal" African heroes. He claims that King Djoser, second king of the Third Dynasty, patron of Imhotep, builder of the Sakkara pyramid, was not Black although his statue shows him to have full lips, flat nose, and protruding lower jaw. Again, as Cheikh Anta Diop argued in *The African Origin of Civilization*, the falsification of African history has been a long tradition in European scholarship. Clearly if "flat nose" is not a marker for an African and an "aquiline nose" is not a marker, then what is a marker for Tiffany? The fact is that the African leaders of ancient Egypt were born long before there is any history of Whites moving out of Europe.

But the Whites are not the only naysayers of the intellectual line pursued by Cheikh Anta Diop, some notable African writers like Messay Kebede (2004) have written in a Eurocentric vein about Diop's work, going so far as to quote the weak and non sequitur arguments of JeanSuret-Canale who claims:

> If Sheikh Anta Diop jeers with reason at such European scholars", who, through unadmitted racial prejudice, have tried to 'whiten' ancient Egypt at all costs, then he himself falls into the same trap in seeking to 'blacken' at all costs, and to give a 'Negro' origin to

the civilizations of the Sumerians, Carthaginians . . . Bretons'
(quoted from Wauthier, 1964: 23–24).

The problem with this statement is that it flies in the face of centuries of European scholarship about Africa. It is not possible for us
to gloss over Suret-Canale's use of the expression "unadmitted racial
prejudice" and assume that since it was unadmitted it did not exist.
For even if it were not a self conscious racism the very society,
schools, institutions, philosophical groups, and orientations of the
European, particularly during a period of conquest, produced writers who thought of themselves as "superior" to Africans.

But Kebede has granted Suret-Canale too much space in his por-
trayal of the attacks on Diop and the space haunts both Kebede and
Suret-Canale. When Kebede continues with Suret-Canale's assault
on Diop, he has the White historian saying that the Egyptian population in the past was no different than it is today. In fact, ". . .
thousands of perfectly preserved mummies as well as skeletons,
leaves no doubt at all on this point. . . . The truth is that in the past,
as today, there was more or less pronounced miscegenation with the
black population of the Upper Nile (such interbreeding also takes
place in the opposite direction via the infiltration of white elements
into Nubia). There are, and there always have been, Negro elements
in Egypt, and even possibly Negro dynasties ruling over a white
population" (Wauthier, 1979).

There are many errors and much nonsense in what Suret-Canale
has written and the unfortunate turn of events is that Kebede seems
not to know what is wrong with the statement. He gives it promi-
nence in his argument as a sure "hammerblow" to Diop but it only
serves to show the inadequacy of the arguments against Diop's position. Let us make a point by point analysis of what we have in these
statements in order to see more clearly the errors. In the first place,
Diop does not try to "blacken" the ancient Egyptians at all costs. He

is talking and writing about an African people, not a European people. There are no descendants of Germans, French, or English in ancient Egypt. The people are neither Aryans, nor Nordics, nor Alpines; they are Black in the way that we understand Blackness to mean people with wooly hair and very dark skin. These are the features of the ancient Egyptians. They are not anything other than Black; they are not Chinese or Greek. As Africans who had "black skin and wooly hair" according to those who saw them and recorded what they saw in antiquity, they were the ancient Egyptians. No one reported seeing any blondes or redheads in ancient Egypt. This is a fact; it is not hearsay. Except for the period of Greek rule during the time of the Ptolemies, Egyptian rulers were Black. There is no proof whatsoever that any of the Egyptians prior to the conquest of Alexander were Whites. So Diop is right and Suret-Canale is wrong on the question of the Blackness of the ancient Egyptians.

The argument that Diop (1974:118–119) makes about the Carthagenians is clearly a historical account. It is important to quote Diop at length on this point:

> Founded on the African coast circa 814 B.C., Carthage was one of the last Phoenician colonies. Since 1450 B.C., white Libyans, people of the sea, Rebou, had invaded North Africa west of Egypt. Before the founding of Carthage they had time to scatter all along the coast, toward the west, as Herodotus reports. The hinterland of Carthage was then inhabited by indigenous Blacks who had been there throughout Antiquity, and by white Libyan tribes. Crossbreeding occurred gradually, as in Spain, and the Carthaginians, both common people and elite, were evidently Negroid. We need not insist on the fact that the Carthaginian general, Hannibal, who barely missed destroying Rome and who is considered one of the greatest military leaders of all time, was Negroid. It can be said that, with his defeat, the supremacy of the Negro or Negroid world ended.

The issue of Carthage is quite simply an issue of Europe seeking to claim every achievement of Africans as European achievements. There is no way that one can stretch the history of Carthage to claim that Hannibal was a European or an Asian! He was clearly an African, born in Africa of African parentage, although he may have had some traces of a Phoenician, that is, Southwest Asian ancestry. But after the founding of the city, the Phoenicians did not constantly supply Carthage with human resources; Africa did. By the time of Hannibal, the Great, Phoenicia had spent its population stream into Africa and it would rise no more. By Hannibal's time, Carthage was fundamentally a Black civilization.

It does not suffice us to go further because the work of Messay Kebede makes its pitch to become a part of Western philosophy, not really to interrogate Africa's quest for a philosophy of decolonization. It is as if Kebede has given up hope without ever trying to see that the Afrocentric response to environmental, conceptual, and economic issues is the only way that the continent can be free enough to operate on the basis of its own will. This is the lesson of history that is right in front of him. Indeed, had Kebede read Diop more closely he would have discovered that the issue which lurks in the back of Kebede's writings—that is, what ever happened to Blacks if it is true that we once ruled the world?—had already been confronted. Diop (1974:156) posed it this way.

> If Blacks created Egyptian civilization, how can we explain their present decline? That question makes no sense, for we could say as much about the Fellahs and Copts, who are supposed to be the direct descendants of the Egyptians and who, today, are at the same backward stage as other Blacks, if not more so. Nevertheless, this does not excuse us from explaining how the technical, scientific, and religious civilization of Egypt was transformed as it adjusted to new conditions in the rest of Africa (1974:156).

Of course, this argument and the subsequent positions taken by Diop escape the sight of Kebede. He rather seeks, in his work, to cast shadows in the direction of Diop rather than to engage him fully. This is unfortunate because he would have learned from the experience and received a considerable shot in the arm of standing against the falsification of African history.

Diop explained that the successive migrations of Africans from the Nile Valley meant that people were inhabiting various areas of the continent at an early time. He says that a profusion of temples and obelisks are found in Nubia and Ethiopia, and especially in the Meroitic part of Sudan. He (Ibid:157) writes that,

> It is in the Meroitic Sudan, Sennar, that temples and pyramids abound. Thus, place names have been falsified to provide a more or less Oriental and discreetly Asiatic origin by way of the Bab el Mandeb for Negro-Egyptian civilization. In reality we must react against a whole terminology. Chamites, Hamites, Oriental and Ethiopian, and even African are, in modern historical writing, euphemisms enabling one to speak of Negro-Sudanese-Egyptian civilization without using the term "Negro" or "Black."

Diop laid down a strong position on the crude falsifications against Africa. He was convinced that the White scholars who had written history could not tell African history correctly. They had taken in too many negatives about the people and the continent and could only produce gross misinterpretations of what they saw, read, or researched.

Therefore, Diop (Ibid:xv–xvii) outlined his positions on ancient Egypt, Blackness, and the future of Africa by referring to ten basic arguments:

1. The ancient Egyptians who built the pyramids were Blacks and Ancient Egypt was a Negro civilization.

2. Anthropologically and culturally speaking, the Semitic world was born during protohistoric times from the mixture of white-skinned and black-skinned people in western Asia. This is why an understanding of the Mesopotamian Semitic world, Judaic or Arabic, requires constant reference to the underlying Black reality.

3. The triumph of the monogenetic thesis of the origin of humanity compels one to admit that all races descended from the Black race.

4. It is possible to write a history of Africa free of mere chronology, but infused with ideas, laws, and the evolution of sociopolitical structures.

5. It is important to define an image of modern Africa that is reconciled to its past.

6. Once the perspectives accepted until now by official sciences have been reversed, the history of humanity will become clear and the history of Africa can be written. But any undertaking in this field that adopts compromise as its point of departure as if it were possible to split the difference or provide half the truth would run the risk of producing nothing but alienation. Clearly, only loyal, determined struggle to destroy cultural aggression and bring out the truth, whatever it may be, is revolutionary and consonant with real progress.

7. Modern Black literature will remained minor until Black African authors pose the problem of man's fate which is the major theme of human letters.

8. There are numerous features common to Black African civilization.

9. African languages can express modern philosophic and scientific thought and African culture will not be taken seriously until their utilization in education becomes a reality.

10. Efforts of scholars working on pre-Columbian relations between Africa and America are important and laudatory.

Maghan Keita (2000) has argued that Africans and African-Americans have always expressed important ideas about the place of Egypt and Ethiopia in the ancient world. In his book, *Race and the Writing of History*, Keita is concerned with the intellectual history of the idea of Afrocentricity in a much more important way than other historians. He believes that race plays a major role in interpretation of events and personalities. Among the conclusions of his work, therefore, is that most White historians have used Blackness in a negative way when writing about ancient history. He also believes that racism has prevented Whites from taking seriously the work of Black historians. What he does not say, but what Diop implies in all of his work, is that White scholarship would find it difficult to take Black writing seriously when Black scholars, who are committed to truth and science, are engaged in the process of disproving the interpretations of White history about Black people. Perhaps one of the most significant observations in Keita's work is that Black scholars must be engaged in corrective historiography while writing history. This is why Cheikh Anta Diop thought it important to "cleanse" the language of history as he wrote history. One cannot refer to African people as "primitives" who live in "huts" and then go on to talk intelligently about the philosophical systems of the African people. One must deal with the fact that racism permeates the entire Western process of education and training.

CHAPTER 5

UNITY AND RENAISSANCE: EXTENDING DIOP'S VIEW

In the *Cultural Unity of Black Africa,* Cheikh Anta Diop expounds on the Pan-African vision of Kwame Nkrumah and others who had long argued for a united continent. The idea of a United States of Africa was grounded in the best political and economic arguments for unity. Diop was clear in his determination that the economic, commercial and resource ties of the African continent were such that it would be an easy task to bring about a perfect African political union.

Cheikh Anta Diop's Pan-African spirit comes out clearly in *Towards the African Renaissance: Essays in Culture and Development.* This work is generated from the essays that he wrote during the time he was a student in Paris and when he returned to Dakar. He sought to write a book that would speak to the common person about the realities of African culture and development. I sense that Diop was tired of the European consultants on development coming to Africa with their schemes on how things should be on the continent. Thus, he organized the book in an accessible way. One does not have to be a scholar to understand the point being made about the necessity of African cultural unity. Cheikh Anta Diop wrote many of the pieces as a passionate defender of African pride and one can tell that he is deeply committed to the future of the continent.

One is introduced in the first two chapters to the Diopian idea of linguistic relations between the African languages. This is an early indication of Diop's commitment to explore the common elements in African societies by using language as a tool for research. Since linguistic analysis combines lexical and phonological elements with syntactical aspects of language, one sees how Diop used semantic articulations and various analogies to demonstrate that the languages have more in common than meets the eye. He examines Wolof and other languages, such as Djola, Peul and Serer. Unquestionably when one reads the work it is easy to see that African languages are clearly more closely related to each other than it seems at first.

By the third chapter of the book we are aware of Diop's key question. He asks, when can we speak of an African renaissance? There is nothing that dominates his work as his desire to see Africa rise from the sleep produced by 500 years of falsification of African history. He wants to see the renaissance in every field and at all levels and this is the central desire of his work. One way to achieve this purpose is to develop the indigenous languages. Diop argues that it is a prerequisite for a real African renaissance. No people have ever achieved a renaissance using some body else's language. In order for it to be a true renaissance we must begin the process of respecting each other's languages, using these languages, and teaching them in schools. Diop (1963:38) writes that "The African is forced to make double efforts: to assimilate the meaning of words and then, through a second intellectual effort, to capture the reality expressed by the words."

One of the ways that the renaissance will happen is when African writers start writing in African languages and having those languages translated into the other non-African languages. The task for the African writers is to write for the African audience and to create a strong sense of the possible among the general readership of Africans. The question really is, who is the writer writing for? The necessity for political education is the key to the renaissance. As the Afrocentrists say, it is necessary to raise the consciousness of the people before we can bring on the renaissance. Thus, Diop makes recommendations for language policy, relationships between African intellectuals, and the need to convene meetings where the intellectuals identify the problems preventing the renaissance and move to see it come to life. It can be accomplished but it will depend upon the African writer taking the leadership to promote political education. He understands that in order for Africans to achieve the future, that is to bring on the renaissance, it will be necessary to ask the linguists and policy makers to avoid easy solutions and to work to change the condition of our people for the best through upgrading all national languages.

Diop was also clear that Africa had to develop its own political ideology, not be a receiver of the ideology of another people. This was a necessary activity before there could be a positive renaissance. To have a rebirth it is important that we understand the contemporary plight of African people. Diop understood that plight and suggested that an African political ideology would be a way to reorganize and create awareness about Africa. Unfortunately, many Africans having been given a negative image of Africa by Europeans have little or no real and positive conception of the continent's history or experiences. So Diop calls upon all Africans to take their place in the renaissance. It does not matter whether the people were of the lower or higher strata of the socio-political spectrum, Diop argued that they had to take up their responsibility. Clearly, there are some people today who argue that he should not have spoken so definitely about the need for Africans to take their roles. The postmodern idea is to insist that individualism is the principal aim of human life and that any collective work or attitude is really about putting in place some one else's idea about what we are to do.

However, I am of the opinion that had Africa had more leaders, intellectual and political, like Diop we would be farther along in the renaissance. He (1963:48) was convinced that "there exists a capitalist exploitation which is the cause of all our misery and which cannot stop without the total annihilation of colonialism." Diop is constructing a consciousness of conflict and opposing camps, and his idea is to join coalition with coalition, and to confront the imperial powers of the Western world with African unity. It is necessary to unmask the African leaders and elite groups who mask as supporters of Africa but who in reality are in an unholy alliance with the enemies of Africa. So Diop has now claimed that we must have an ideological and a political consciousness. Actually, it is the ideology, obviously an Afrocentric ideology, that must guide the great spirit of Africa. More important, we must understand that the alliance with a capitalist Europe is always to the advantage of Europe; it is not made to support Africa or Africans.

Diop knew, as we all know, that you cannot have any renaissance without economic independence. Africa must rise to the challenge of economic renewal and this means that the great wealth of the continent must be used for the interest of Africa. Diop claimed that Africa's wealth must be aware of its economic condition. He (1963:97) understood as he said that "one finds a numerically weak group [Africa] lacking in all the advantages of modern life, but sitting on fabulous wealth. On the other hand is an economically poor group [the West] which is gifted with all it takes to take risks." It is also true that the West has been quick to use force and might to bring about its own ends. This is a clear pattern of Western behavior in world affairs for the past five hundred years. Thus, Diop could point out that the risks the West is prepared to take include exploitation and extermination of "natives" (what the British Americans did to Indians or what the British Australians did to the black fellows in Australia) and in what Diop refers to as the "policy of infiltration."

There are many African and African American scholars who see a connection between Diop's arguments and those of intellectual activists such as Frantz Fanon and Walter Rodney. But it is clear that the connections are based on political objectives. These writers are concerned about the political, economic, and mental liberation of Africa. Fanon's (1963) work, *The Wretched of the Earth,* was in the tradition of Diop's analysis of the West. In addition, Fanon had written a series of articles that were published as a book, *Toward the African Revolution* (1967), which also fit in this framework of analysis. A connection can be made also, with Walter Rodney's classic text, *How Europe Underdeveloped Africa,* where Rodney deals with the economic destruction of Africa by Europe. The style of argument begins with examples and concrete realities and then suggests that those are the methods of operation of Western exploitation. If you take any country in Africa, you will see that the wealth, especially the mineral wealth, is enough to feed the people and to give them a reasonable style of life. However, with the exploitation of the minerals by Western companies, the African people do not often share in the wealth being generated by their natural resources. Diop cites, among others, several methods used in South Africa by the old minority regime to undermine the African people:

119

1. The White regime encouraged immigration of Nazis exclusively: Germans, Dutch etc. The French, Italians and even British were originally refused immigration rights for not being sufficiently racist. The aim of the apartheid regime was to make the White population dominant in terms of its racist attitude.
2. The White regime sought to increase its capacity to absorb foreign White elements while decreasing its attractiveness to foreign black elements.
3. The White regime practiced a policy of racial segregation in all aspects of existence (apartheid), hence a series of laws whose vile and obscene nature was to make Africans grovel in a subhuman existence due to food scarcity in a country that is one of the richest agricultural regions in the world.

4. The White regime wanted to deny Africans any higher education, or if they were educated, to give them an apartheid education which would deny the history of African people.

In this book Diop suggests that the West and European powers
used policies that would allow them to exploit Africa's resources for
the benefit of Europe. The reason for economic exploitation is
because Africa has vast reserves in hydraulic energy, uranium and
other minerals whereas "Europe is an empty box" (1963:117). Diop
believed that Africa, not Saudi Arabia, was the energy center of the
world, and its economic independence from the West adds another
requirement for renaissance. To show his Pan-African understanding Diop calls for an organic relationship between Africa and the
Caribbean. This is a remarkable vision because it sees the possibility
of an Africa union of economic influence.

The last three chapters (9, 10 & 11) in the book underscore what
Diop has been writing about in the earlier chapters. This is probably
because of the collective character of the book. He writes of the need
for linguistic, political and economic consciousness among Africans
and a cultural unity that is deeply rooted in African history. For example, he argues that ancient Africa has a culture of matriarchy, as
opposed to Western patriarchy, which needs to be revived as Africa
approaches the renaissance. I take it that Diop's vision is what is
driving the African Union's historic call for an international meeting
of African intellectuals in 2004. Under the leadership of Presidents
Abdoulaye Wade of Senegal, Thabo Mbeki of South Africa, and J.
Chissano of Mozambique, African leaders have called for the comple-
tion of this part of Diop's vision. President Wade going so far as to say,
"If Africa became a nation tomorrow, I would gladly accept to be governor of Senegal." Indeed, Diop mandates intellectuals and politicians
"to study the past not for their pleasure but to learn useful lessons." A
lesson that we should learn according to Diop (1963:138) is that:

Our history has been falsified to suit a certain cause, that our traditions have been misrepresented and our culture ridiculed in order
to arrange our allegiance to the wishes of the different European
countries which had shared our land amongst themselves.

Diop's *Towards the African Renaissance* is a blueprint for an archi-
tecton of African revival. It is this work that will serve as a model for
African countries to regain a sense of dignity. This book represents
a vision, a beautiful vision, of Africa in its glory. This is not a
romantic book, but one based on understanding the material conditions that exist in the African world. It will help establish the
grounds for Africa unity, but this unity will have a concrete ideological foundation.

Diop sees our consciousness and political education about the
colonial formulations as necessary to bring about the renaissance.
Diop (1963:71) maintains: "We are therefore obliged to review our
strategy and tactics in order to adapt them to this new situation if
we desire to enhance our chances of success." What is so creative
about the blueprint for renaissance is that Diop recognizes the
inherent process of checking to see that the actions for renaissance
match the realities. He is a political strategist as well as a philosopher of culture.

Furthermore, this book provides the reader with a reason to
believe in the future of Africa. However, the reader is asked to participate in that future by being fully engaged in the political consciousness and political education necessary to bring about the
renaissance. It is only normal and natural that the oppressed people
should revolt and throw off the shackles. Every work by Diop is
another assault on the fundamental issue that threatens African
revivalism. He is a master at convincing the reader of the possibility
of the renaissance. Few Continental African writers understood the
racist nature of America more than Diop. He writes in the chapter,

"Alarm in the Tropics", about America's fundamentally racist society and reiterates his position that the country is racist to its core because all classes of Whites practice White racial domination. There is no class of White people that is immune from the racism that permeates so many institutions in the nation.

Finally, Diop returns to his use of linguistic inquiry as a tool to address the issue of race. It is his intention to illustrate the fact that linguistic and cultural diversity is a result of isolation and migration. This is true for all societies but it is often forgotten in the discussions around African diversity. Migration is the most dynamic factor in diversity. Isolation brought about by migration is a second force for diversity. He shows that the Wolof language comes about through migration and not by race alone. The idea that there is a racial component to language is not scientific, but what is scientific is the idea that people who migrate to a certain region will carry with them aspects of their earlier civilization. There is no such thing as a Yoruba or Wolof or Akan race. Indeed Diop (1963:31) concludes: "The Wolof race, in the conventional sense, is a myth." Diop wants the reader to see that the attitude of the capitalists is to continue the colonial relationship with the African people. He seeks to convince Africans that unity is necessary and possible. *Towards the African Renaissance* is one of the clearest political mandates from an intellectual and ranks with Fanon's best works in this genre.

There were three questions that presented themselves to him for examination: (1) why did the Europeans seek to place Africans outside of history; (2) why did the Europeans seek to whiten the ancient Black Egyptians; and (3) how to recover the best of the classical and African culture, Kemet, to improve and enhance the life and future of African people? These three questions would be the driving issues throughout his career. He would visit and revisit them many times with different research tools. Nothing could deter him from his search for answers to the age-old questions that had plagued the African world. Africa had to be free of colonialism he reasoned but the only way that it would occur would be if a social scientist, using the best academic tools, could undermine the lie upon which the colonial empire was built. Diop was, therefore, first of all, an activist who was prepared to demonstrate against the French colonial power while studying at their institutions.

Diop had joined the student movement and became one of the leaders in the political agitation. As a student in 1951 he helped to organize the First African Students Pan-African Congress. Diop was made the Secretary-General of the Rassemblement Democratique Africain (RDA) between 1951 and 1953. But with all of his political work, he never forgot his principal mission which was to show the basis of the French occupation, and all colonial occupation in Africa, as a racism designed to subdue, exploit and create a negative impression of Africa to justify this. Thus, he was willing to tackle the major scholars in the European world after studying various subjects, including history, linguistics, mathematics, and sociology. Diop would carry the fight to the solemn halls of the Sorbonne. His initial doctoral dissertation submitted to the faculty of the Sorbonne in 1951 was rejected as being unfounded. Its major thesis was that the ancient Egyptian civilization was a Black civilization. The French faculty could not bear to see an African challenge the staple diet of White supremacy so logically. Although rejected by the Sorbonne the dissertation was published by Alioune Diop's publishing house, *Presénce Africaine*, and immediately became a popular work among intellectuals. The title of the publication was *Nations negres et culture,* later to be translated in English in 1974 as *The African Origin of Civilization*. In 1956 he participated in the First World Congress of Black Writers in Paris and in 1959 he went to Rome for the second such congress. Soon two more attempts to gain the doctorate were made and finally in 1960, a full nine years after the first attempt, Diop was able to sit with a committee of the faculty at the

Sorbonne and carry his argument that the ancient Egyptians were black-skinned people. He further argued that Europeans had falsified the information concerning the African origin of civilization.

He published two additional books out of his research. They were the *Cultural Unity of Black Africa* and *Precolonial Black Africa*. Both of these books sought to show that the Africans of Egypt and the Africans of West Africa were of the same basic culture. Furthermore, they were to demonstrate that the pre-colonial culture of Africa was developed, sophisticated, and had a political maturity that even Europe did not know. Both works added to his esteem and made him a household name among the Pan-African intellectuals. By 1966, the First World Black Festival of Arts and Culture held in Dakar could name Cheikh Anta Diop and W. E. B. Du Bois as the greatest thinkers to impact on the African world. Generally thought of as redirecting the historiography of the entire African continent, scholars normally think of Diop as being the most significant thinker to emerge from the African continent. Certainly the reach of his work is the most international.

The publication of *The African Origin of Civilization: Myth or Reality* was a major English language achievement. Scholars who could not read him in French rushed to purchase his book. Soon Diop was the most talked about Black scholar in the United States of America. Led by John Henrik Clarke, a chorus of scholars began to raise the name and work of Diop throughout the English speaking world. Everyone knew something about Diop but few had any deep understanding of the tremendous work that he had done. Most of his books and articles remain untranslated from the French. Nevertheless, enough had been done with five of his books in English to characterize him as a major voice in world scholarship. The same year, 1974, that *The African Origin of Civilization* appeared in English, Diop joined with the young scholar Theophile Obenga of the Congo-Brazzaville to argue the Blackness of the ancient Egyptians at the UNESCO Conference on the Peopling of Egypt in Cairo. They were overwhelmingly successful in their arguments.

In 1981, Diop's work, *Civilization or Barbarism: An Authentic Anthropology,* was released in English. This work added to the distinctions that Diop had already amassed as scholars concluded that he had written the most profound arguments in support of the African origin of civilization of any African scholar. When he went home to his "village" he had achieved the stature of a modern Imhotep. He had been cited widely, quoted often, and feted in the major academic institutions of the world. His work had received attention belatedly in his own home; nevertheless, his work as the Director of the Radiocarbon Laboratory of the Fundamental Institute of Black Africa brought him in contact with many people. This is where I found him in 1980 when I stopped in his office.

THE DEVELOPMENT OF DIOPIAN PROJECTS

As mentioned above, Diop has had a profound influence on the intellectual and practical work of scholars, activists and activist-scholars on the African continent and in the Diaspora. The discourse he initiated on ancient Egypt influenced both senior and young scholars interested in ancient Egyptian studies. Among the Africans in the United States no one has done more than Clyde Ahmad Winters (1985, 1989) to deal with the fundamental question of languages as theorized by Diop. He has sought to confirm the theories of Diop in relationship to the genetic unity of the Egyptian, Black African, Elamite, Sumerian and Dravidian languages. Winters has spent many years studying languages in order to demonstrate the unity of ancient, old and new world Black civilizations. This has led him to work to decipher writing systems used by these Africans. Other scholars in the United States such as Chancellor Williams, author of *The Destruction of Black Civilization,* Yosef ben-Jochannon,

Asa Hilliard, Jacob Carruthers, and John Jackson have popularized many of the ideas found in Diop.

Chancellor Williams was a professor at Howard University when he wrote his important book, *The Destruction of Black Civilization*, which became a popular work in the genre of correcting African history. Williams contended that the European people had deliberately falsified the record of Africans in order to bring about the destruction of African civilization. Yosef ben-Jochannan emerged in the 1960s as one of the leading popularizers of the African origin of civilization based on his many years of living in Egypt and Ethiopia. Using his base from Africa, ben-Jochannon studied African history and culture and ultimately found himself in the position to write about Egypt in ways that touched the common man. He studied history and cultural anthropology to perfect his knowledge of the African past. Influenced by Cheikh Anta Diop, John Henrik Clarke, William Leo Hansberry, and Arthur Schomburg, ben-Jochannon wrote three major works, *Black Man on the Nile and His Family*, *The African Origin of the Major Western Religions*, and *Africa: Mother of Western Civilization*. Dr. Ben, as he is affectionately called, has become an icon among people of New York because he attacked the European scholars who argued that Egypt was not Black. In this line of attack, ben-Jochannon, although not a scientist in his thinking, did a lot to create an interest in the African past.

The late Jacob Carruthers was a promoter of Diop's ideas in a religious sense. He developed an institution based on the Kemetic ideals first introduced in the works of Diop. On the other hand, Diop, himself, never allowed his scholarship to mix with religion. The two were separate and this distinction was maintained in all of his works. One could not call Diop a religious promoter or a campaigner for any particular religious expression, if anything, he remained a free-thinker. Asa Hilliard, an educator, who re-introduced George G. M. James to the American public when he

126

sponsored the re-issuing of *Stolen Legacy*, is an avid student of Diop. Charles Finch has done more than any other African person to uncover the role of ancient Africa in medicine. He is a serious student of Diop and classical Africa and has demonstrated in his work a commitment to excellence.

Maulana Karenga (2006; 1990; 1984) is arguably the foremost Afrocentric Ancient Egyptian Studies scholar. An eminent authority on *Maat*, the central moral and spiritual category of ancient Egypt, he has defined the themes of modern Maatian philosophical discourse, excavated the relevant intellectual concepts and categories, and uncovered the hidden issues that support the Western hegemony. He has done this with an extensive critical examination of the moral and ethical values of the ancient Africans of Egypt (Karenga, 2006). This is important because he has turned the discourse from anthropology to substantive intellectual ideas of ancient Africa.

A scholar who has done more than anyone else to continue the work of Cheikh Anta Diop is Théophile Obenga (1992b, 1995). He was born in Congo, Brazzaville, Equatorial Africa and was educated in Belgium, France, and the United States. He is considered one of the foremost students and followers of Cheikh Anta Diop. In the preface to Obenga's book *Africa in Antiquity* (1973:vi), Diop wrote: "Obenga is a polyvalent scholar with a threefold training as a philosopher, historian and linguist and knowing Greek, Latin, French, English, Italian, and practicing Arabic and Syriac. More importantly, he is the first Black African of his generation able to read the pharaonic language in the texts: he holds a degree in Egyptology and is a member of the Societe Francaise d'Egyptologie." During the UNESCO Colloquium on "The Peopling of Ancient Egypt and the Decipherment of Meroitic Writing" held in Cairo (January 28–February 3, 1974), Diop and Obenga distinguished themselves by presenting brilliant discourses on the Blackness of the ancient Egyptians. This intellectual demonstration was considered a landmark in African studies and their appearance together at the Cairo conference anticipated the decline of White cultural imperialism over Africa's antiquity. Black Egypt was returned to its rightful place in history and the time had come for Black scholars to stand against the attempt to whiten ancient Egypt.

Under Marien NGouabi's government in the Congo, Obenga was Director of the Ecole Normale Superieure where he created an outstanding method for teaching African historiography and later became Minister for Foreign Affairs. He then took the post of Director General of the International Center for Bantu Studies, the only high-tech African-oriented database and cultural center of its kind focusing on the Egypto-Bantu world and head-quartered in Libreville, Gabon. Obenga (1978b) is the author of numerous scholarly works, many of which were published by *Présence Africaine* including, in particular, *Precolonial Central Africa, Zaire: Traditional Civilizations and Modern Culture. Stele for the Future (poetry), For A New History, Traditional Literature of the Mbochi*, and *The Bantu: Languages, Peoples and Civilizations*. He has had a remarkable career in the United States joining with me this author at Temple University in the early 1990s to teach the Egyptian Language at the only doctoral granting department in African and African American Studies. Soon thereafter he was called back to Congo to join the government as Minister of Industry and Technology. After a short stint in government he became Professor and Head of the Department of Black Studies at the San Francisco State University in California. He has maintained his ties to the ANKH organization in Paris as well as to the Cheikh Anta Diop Conference in Philadelphia, the Association for the Study of Classical African Civilizations, and other groups.

Since the death of Cheikh Anta Diop there have been a number of schools developed around his work. One such school is gathered around Theophile Obenga and Cheikh M'Backe Diop and others in

Paris. This cadre has a strong practical dimension to their work. They are all scientists in various fields—astronomy, nuclear, computers, information, and so forth. An architect, Salomon Mezepo, is a publisher with this group and has founded *Menaibuc Editions*, in much the same way as Alioune Diop founded *Presénce Africaine* during the Negritude movement. The Paris group also publishes a journal of Kemetic studies called *ANKH*. The project which they have carried out is around the dissemination of the *Mdw Ntr*. They have an active group of teachers who are derived from this group of scientists that continue to make progress, not just in teaching the ancient language of Egypt, but in producing new articles and research on Egypt.

A second group is identified with the Association for the Study of Classical African Civilization that was originally founded by Maulana Karenga and Jacob Carruthers (Karenga, 2002). It is currently led by Nzingha Ratibisha, Asa Hilliard, Leonard and Rosalind Jeffries. Theophile Obenga is also associated with this group. ASCAC began as group with the aim of engaging in original research in the field. This is a promise that remains unfulfilled. A third group associated with the National Association of Kawaida Organizations is supported by the intellectual work of Maulana Karenga. It is essentially concerned with the ethical dimensions to the ancient texts of Egypt. This school is devoted to the study and dissemination of information on the meaning of the texts, the substance of the philosophy, and the definitions and interpretations of *Maat*. The work that Karenga wants to see done is with the living words of the texts (Karenga, 2006). He asks often for scholars who will interrogate the texts for ethical and social content rather than use them as artifacts.

Finally, there is a Diopian school associated with Molefi Kete Asante, Ama Mazama, and Maulana Karenga, around the Cheikh Anta Diop Conference that meets each year in Philadelphia. This conference, coordinated by Ana Yenenga, is the single most important meeting of scholars in the field of Diopian research. Each year scores of young and senior scholars gather to present their work and publications for critical commentary to an audience of hundreds of serious scholars. The ubiquitous Theophile Obenga is also associated with this group having been one of its founders, along with Freya Rivers and Molefi Kete Asante, of the Association of Nubian Kemetic Heritage, A Scientifc Institute, while cruising up the Nile River in 1996. In 2000, the ANKH Institute took over the operation of the Cheikh Anta Diop International Conference due to conflict with Temple University. The organization has grown immensely since becoming independent. I am certain that I have missed some groups or schools that have developed because of Diop; they, too, represent his legacy and he has become a part of the heritage of all scholars dedicated to the proposition that falsifications about African history and culture should not be able to continue without challenge.

Mozer (2002:10) recognized that the impact of Diop's work was first felt among the Anglo American communities. Although Diop wrote in French and his works were translated into English, he is now discussed in many languages. However, Mozer is correct to argue that it is important for scholars to engage the intellectual ideas of Diop. Indeed, the Diopian moment is one in which the destiny of contemporary science, particularly regarding the African world, is deeply ingrained in new interpretations. I see the Diopian moment as one of the most creative in the history of African studies because it has generated more published materials, created more intellectual spaces, opened new concepts to analysis, and provided the African scholar with a leadership role in the interrogation of his or her own cultural history.

This is a remarkable turn about from the days when European scholars dominated the discussion of all African history, including African antiquity. It is easy to understand how Mozer sees this moment as one in which there is a retotalization of knowledge around ancient Egypt, not a retotalization in the "sens cumulative du terme", but in the sense of an extreme elaboration of the complexity of the subject (Ibid:11). Things are not as cut and dried in ancient Egyptian studies as when the White scholars had the field to themselves. In fact, it has been entirely different since the appearance of Diop's *Nations Negres et Culture*. Diop maintained the necessity for the independence of the African thinker as much as he fought for the political independence of the continent. His first major work, Black Nations and Culture was subtitled "The Antiquity of Black Egypt and the Cultural Problems of Contemporary Black Africa."

There is no question in my mind that Diop saw the contemporary problems of Africa through the lens of the ancient world. The result of a lack of historical consciousness was a death of memory, a truncated vision, and a distorted reality that could only lead to more death. Ancient historical consciousness was connected to modern cultural realities. If Africans did not see themselves as the masters of their own destinies then it was likely that they had no idea of what Africans had done in the past. If Africans believed the falsehood that had been spread by Europe that there were no ancient African civilizations then Africans could never conceive of Egypt as being Black. The problem, and Diop saw it and did something about it, was that the information that had been disseminated to the schools, universities and in the text books was wrong. Others had seen the same problems but only in Diop did the concern and the intellect combine in the same individual, one with will, determination, and courage to produce a book that laid out new epistemological directions.

In my judgment it is Diop's command of the theoretical and practical bases of archaeology, physics, history, linguistics, chemistry, and paleontology that gave him such a wide range of interdisciplinary legitimacy. As to his language skills, he was reasonably proficient in Greek, English, Latin, Coptic, and Middle Egyptian. He was expert in Wolof, Pular, French and several other languages.

Indeed, he spoke classical Wolof, that is, without French interjections. It is this interdisciplinary competence which prepared him well to lead the epistemological battle against all forms of Eurocentric intellectual racism.

Mozer speaks of Diop responding to the crisis in modern history, a sort of urgency for the voice of Africa to be heard in its own cause and in its own court. How can one really examine African history and culture without delving into the substance of that history and culture? The only response is the way Diop attempted to unify the fields of molecular biology, nuclear physics, linguistics, and anthropology in his effort to render complete his thesis that the ancient pharaonique Egyptians were Black and the founders of human civilization. Thus, Mozer (2002:15) could write *"C'est donc a contre-courant des discours de la regionalisation et des epistemologies du moindre que Diop va, de bonne heure, entrouvrir les horizons egyptiens d'une pensee don't la complexite permet de renouveler l'equilibre d'une science rigoureusement attachee a l'ethique de la recherché."* (It is therefore against the discourse about regionalization and against diminishing epistemologies that Diop will, quite early, open up the Egyptian horizon of a thought that is complex enough to rejuvenate a science rigorously attached to research ethics.) (trans. A. Mazama).

It has been left to Maulana Karenga to navigate the ethical and moral territory of ancient Egypt in the light of Diop. In fact, he has addressed the question Diop raised in his last book concerning the possibility and necessity of Africa providing a world-encompassing philosophy that provides an ethical framework for engaging modern moral and social issues. In his classic tome, *Maat: The Moral Ideal in Ancient Egypt*, he reconstructs the Maatian ethical tradition and demonstrates its value for philosophic reflection and critical engagement with the pressing issues of our time.

The great lesson of Cheikh Anta Diop's intellectual life is that synthesis should not be postponed indefinitely. His argument against fragmentation brought about by analysis is relevant and reflective of the oratorical pronouncement of Leonard Jeffries that there should never be "a paralysis brought about by analysis." In Diop's (1974:275) own words, "the difference in the intellectual approach of the African and European researcher often causes these misunderstandings in the interpretation of facts and their relative importance. The scientific interests of the European scholar with regard to African data is essentially analytical." While Diop concludes that the African scholar distrusts this fragmentation of the collective historical consciousness into minute facts and details, seeking to synthesize in order to have a fuller, more complete picture, he is certain that the researcher might learn from all forms of knowledge, so long as it does not produce immobility. One must act to humanize the world.

REFERENCES

Adams, William Y. (1984). *Nubia: Corridor to Africa*. Princeton, NJ: Princeton University Press.

Al-Bakri. (1913). *Description de l'Afrique septentrionale* (trans. Slane). Algiers: Typographie Adophe Jourdan.

Anselin, A. (1989). "Pour une morpologie elementaire du negro-africain," *Carbet: Revue Martinique de Sciences Humaines et de Litterature*, no.6

———. (1982). *Le Mythe D' Europe*. Paris: Editions Anthropos.

———. (1992a). "L'ibis du savoir-l'ecriture et le mythe en ancienne Egypte," *ANKH*, no.1.

———. (2000). "Boeufs et Pasteurs-Soudain, Libye, Ancienne Egypt," *Cahiers Caribeens d'Egyptologie*, (February/March).

———. (1992b). *Samba*. Guadeloupe: Editions de L'Unite de Recherche-Action Guadeloupe.

Armstrong, R. G. (1962). "Glottochronology and African linguistics," *Journal of African History*, 3 (2).

Asante, Molefi Kete. (1987). *The Afrocentric Idea*. Philadelphia: Temple University Press.

———. (1988). *Afrocentricity*. Trenton: Africa World Press.

———. (1990). *Kemet, Afrocentricity, and Knowledge*. Trenton: Africa World Press.

———. (1994). *Classical Africa*. Maywood, N.J.: The Peoples Publishing Group, Inc.

Babou, Dame. (2004). "Interview with Molefi Kete Asante," Dakar (May 3).

Baines, J. (1991). "Was Civilization Made in Africa?" *The New York Times Review of Books*, (August 11) 12–13.

Bangura, Ahmed. (2000). *Islam and the West African Novel, Politics of Representation*. London: Rienner Publishers.

Beardsley, Grace M. (1929, 1967). *The Negro in Greek and Roman Civilization.* New York: Russell and Russell.

Ben-Jochannan, Yosef. (1971, 1988). *Africa: Mother of Western Civilization.* Baltimore, MD: Black Classic Press.

———. (1972). *African Origins of the Major Western Religions.* New York: Alkebu-Lan.

Bernal, Martin. (1987). *Black Athena: the Afro Asiatic Roots of Classical Civilization, Volume I: The Fabrication of Ancient Greece, 1875–1985.* New Brunswick: Rutgers University Press.

———. (1991). *Black Athena: the Afro Asiatic Roots of Classical Civilizwation, Volume II: The Archaeological and Documentary Evidence.* New Brunswick: Rutgers University Press.

Blyden, Edward Wilmot. (1887). *Christianity, Islam and the Negro Race.* London: W. B. Whittingham.

Breasted, James H. (1962). *Ancient Records of Egypt: Historical Documents From the Earliest Times to the Persian Conquest.* New York: Russell and Russell.

———. (1930). *The Edwin Smith Surgical Payprus,* Chicago: The University of Chicago Press.

Brodrick, Mary (ed. and trans.). (1892). *Mariette, Outlines of Ancient Egyptian History.* New York: Scribner's Sons.

Browder, Anthony Y. (1992). *Nile Valley Contributions to Civilization: Exploding the Myths, Vol. 1.* (Introduction) John Henrik Clarke. Washington, D.C. Institute of Karmic Guidance.

Brunson, James. (1991). *Predynastic Egypt: An African-centric View.* (Introduction) Runoko Rashidi. Dekalb: Brunson.

Budge, E. A. Wallis. (1977). *The Dwellers on the Nile: The Life, History, Religion and Literature of the Ancient Egyptians.* New York: Dover.

Butler, Alfred J. (1992). *The Arab Invasion of Egypt and the Last Thirty Years of the Roman Dominion.* (Introduction) John Henrik Clarke. Brooklyn: A&B.

Bynon, T. (1978). *Historical Linguistics.* London: Cambridge University Press.

Bynum, Edward Bruce. (1999). *The African Unconscious: Roots of Ancient Mysticism and Modern Psychology.* (Foreword) Linda James Myers. New York: Teachers College.

Crawley, T. (1992). *An Introduction to Historical Linguistics.* Oxford: Oxford University Press.

Carruthers, Jacob H. (1984). *Essays in Ancient Egyptian Studies*. (Foreword) Maulana Karenga. Los Angeles: University of Sankore Press.

———. (1995). *Mdr Ntr: Divine Speech (A Historiographical Reflection on African Deep Thought from the Time of the Pharaohs to the Present)*. (Foreword) John Henrik Clarke. London: Karnak House.

Davidson, Basil. (1973). *The Ages of Man*. London: Macmillan.

Delany, M. R. (1879). *Principia of Ethnology: Origins of Races and Color*. Philadelphia, PA.

Diagne, Pathe. (1981). In J. Ki-Zerbo (ed.), *General History of Africa I: Methodology and African Prehistory*. London: Heinemann Educational Books Ltd.

———. (2002) *Cheikh Anta Diop et L'Afrique dans L'histoire du Monde*, Paris: Sankore.

Diodorus, Siculus. (1738). *Histoire universelle de Diodore de Sicile*. (Traduite en français par M. l'Abbé Terrasson), Amsterdam: J. Wetstein & G. Smith.

Diop, Cheikh Anta. (1974). *The African Origin of Civilization: Myth or Reality*. Westport, Conn.: Lawrence Hill and Company.

———. (1975). *L'Antiquite africaine par l'image, Notes Africaine*, numero special 145–146 (janvier-avril).

———. (1960). *L'Afrique noire precoloniale*. Paris: Présence Africaine.

———. (1967). *Anteriorite des civilizations negres: Mythe ou verite historique?* Paris: Présence Africaine.

———. (1981). *Civilization or Barbarism*. Chicago: Lawrence Hill Books.

———. (1974). *Les fondements economiques et culturels d'un Etat federal d'Afrique*, Paris: Présence Africaine.

———. (1981). "A Methodology for the Study of Migrations," *in African Ethnonyms and Toponyms, UNESCO*. Paris: UNESCO.

———. (1955). *Nations negres et culture*. Paris: Présence Africaine.

———. (1988). *Nouvelles recherches sur l'egyptien ancien et les langues négro-africaine modernes*, Paris: Présence Africane.

———. (1977). *Parentè gènètique de l'egyptien pharaonique et des languues negro-africaines*. Dakar: Institut Fondamental d'Afrique Noire.

———. (1987). *Precolonial Black Africa*. Chicago: Lawrence Hill and Company.

———. (1963). *Toward the African Renaissance*. Paris: Présence Africaine.

———. (1960). *L'Unite culturelle de l'Afrique noire*, Paris: Présence Africaine.

Diop, Cheikh M'Backe. (2003). *Cheikh Anta Diop: L'Homme et L'Oeuvre*. Paris: Présence Africaine

Drake, St. Clair, (1987). *Black Folk Here and There: An Essay in History and Anthropology*, Volume I. Los Angeles: Center for Afro American Studies, University of California.

———. (1990). *Black Folk Here and There: An Essay in History and Anthropology*, Volume II. Los Angeles: Center for Afro American Studies, University of California, Los Angeles.

DuBois, W. E. B. (1971). "The American Negro Intelligentsia," in *Apropos of Africa*, (eds.) Adelaide Hill and Martin Kilson. New York: Anchor Books.

———. (1915). *The Negro*. New York.

———. (1946). *The World and Africa: An Inquiry into the part which Africa has played in World History*. New York: International Publishers.

Ehret, C. (1988). "Language change and the material correlates of language and ethnic shift," *Antiquity,* 62, 564–574.

Ehret, C. & Posnansky (eds.). (1982). *The Archaeological and Linguistic Reconstruction of African History*. Berkeley: University of California Press.

Ela, Jean Marc. (2000). *Cheikh Anta Diop ou L'Honneur de Penser*. Paris: Menaibuc.

Fanon, Frantz. (1967). *Black Skin, White Masks*. New York: Grove Press.

———. (1967). *Toward the African Revolution*. New York: Grove Press.

———. (1963). *Wretched of the Earth*. New York: Grove Press.

Faure, Elie. (1937). *History of Art*. Garden City: Doubleday.

Frobenius, L. (1913). *The Voice of Africa*, 2 volumes. London: Hutchinson & Co.

Gnonsea, Doue. (2003). *Cheikh Anta Diop, Theophile Obenga: Combat pour la Re-naissance Africaine*. Paris: L'Harmattan.

Granville, S. K. R., ed. (1933). *The Legacy of Egypt*. London: Oxford University Press.

Hansberry, William Leo. (1981). *Africa and Africans as Seen by Classical Writers*. Joseph E. Harris (ed.), Washington, D.C.: Howard University Press.

Harris, Joseph, (ed.). (1977). *Africa and Afrians as Seen by Classical Writers: The William Leo Hansberry African History Notebook,* Volume II. Washington, D.C.: Howard University Press.

Hegel, G. (1974). *Lectures on the History of Philosophy*, 3 volumes. (trans. eds.) Haldane and Franes H. Simpson, London: Routledge and Kegan Paul.

Herodotus. (1972). *The Histories*. (Trans.) Aubrey de Selincourt. Rev. ed. Harmonds-worth: Penguin.

Hilliard, Asa G. III. (2002). "The Myth of the Immaculate Conception of Western Civilization," in *Egypt vs. Greece and the American Academy: The Debate Over the Birth of Civilization*. (eds.) Molefi Kete Asante and Ama Mazama. Chicago: African American Images.

———. (1997). *SBA: The Reawakening of the African Mind*. (Foreword) Wade W. Nobles, Gainesville: Makare Books.

Hilliard, Asa G. III, Larry Obadele Williams and Nia Damali, (eds.) (1987). *The Teachings of Ptahhotep: The Oldest Book in the World*. Atlanta: Blackwood Press.

Houston, Drusilla D. (1985). *Wonderful Ethiopians of the Ancient Cushite Empire*. 1926; reprint. Baltimore: Black Classic Press.

Jackson, John G. (1990). *Ages of Gold and Silver and Other Short Sketches of Human History*. (Foreword) Madalyn O'Hair, Austin: American Atheist Press.

James, George G. M. (1954). *Stolen Legacy: The Greeks Were not the Authors of Greek Philosophy, but the People of North Africa Commonly Called the Egyptians*. New York: Philosophical Library.

Jayne, Walter Addison. (1925). *The Healing Gods of Ancient Civilizations*. New Haven: Yale University Press.

Keita., Maghan. (2000). *Race and the Writing of History: Riddling the Sphinx*. New York: Oxford University Press.

Karenga, Maulana. (1990). *The Book of Coming Forth By Day: The Ethics of the Declarations of Innocence*, Los Angeles: University of Sankore Press.

———. (2006). *Maat: The Moral Ideal in Ancient Egypt*. Los Angeles: University of Sankore Press.

———. (1984). *Selections from the Husia: Sacred Wisdom of Ancient Egypt*, Los Angeles: University of Sankore Press.

King, Leophus Taharka. (2004). *Philomythy: Ancient Egyptian Correspondences in Greek Creation Myths*. Unpublished dissertation, Temple University, 2004.

Lichtheim, Miriam. (1975). *Ancient Egyptian Literature: A Book of Readings*, 3 volumes. Berkeley: University of California Press.

Lefkowitz, Mary. (1992). "Not out of Africa," *The New Republic* (February 10) 29–36.

Lewis, R. B. (1844). *Light and Truth, collected from the Bible and the ancient and modern history, containing the universal history of the Colored and Indian race from creation of the world to the present.* Boston: Published by a committee of colored gentlemen, [B. F. Roberts, printer].

Lord, R. (1966). *Comparative Linguistics.* London: St. Paul's House.

Manetho. (1940). (Trans.) W. G. Waddell, Cambridge: Harvard University Press.

Massey, Gerald. (1973). *Ancient Egypt: Light of the World.* New York: Samuel Weiser.

Mazama, Ama (ed.). (2003). *The Afrocentric Paradigm.* Trenton: Africa World Press.

Mozer, Nzue Paulin Carlos. (2002). *Nouvelles Perspectives Epitstemologiques Autour de la Pensee de Cheikh Anta Diop,* Paris: Menaibuc.

Ngom, G. (1986). "Rapports egypte-Afrique noire: aspects linguistiques," *Présence Africaine,* no. 137/138.

Niane, D. T. (ed.) (1984). "Introduction," *General History of Africa IV,* London: Heinemann Educational Books, pp. 1–14.

Obenga, Theophile. (1973). *L'Afrique dans l'antiquite-Egypte pharaonique-Afrique noire.* Paris: Présence Africaine.

———. (1992b). *Ancient Egypt and Black Africa: A Student's Handbook for the Study of Ancient Egypt in Philosophy, Linguistics and Gender Relations,* (ed.) Amon Saba Saakana. London: Karnak House.

———. (1995). *A Lost Tradition: African Philosophy in World History.* Philadelphia: The Source Editions.

———. (1978a). "Africa in Antiquity," *Africa Quarterly,* 18, no. 1, 1–15.

———. (1978b). "The genetic linguistic relationship between Egyptian (ancient Egyptian and Coptic) and modern African languages," in *UNESCO* (ed.), *The Peopling of Ancient Egypt and the deciphering of the Meroitic Script,* Paris: UNESCO, pp. 65–71.

———. (1992a). "Le Chamito-semitique n'existe pas," *ANKH,* No. 1, 51–58.

———. (1993). *Origine commune de l'Egyptien Ancien du Copte et des langues Negro-Africaines,* Modernes. Paris: Editions L'Harmattan.

Olderogge, L. (1981). "Migrations and ethnic and linguistic differentiations," in J. Ki-Zerbo (ed.), *General History of Africa I: Methodology and African History,* Paris: UNESCO, pp. 271–278.

Oldfather, C. H. (trans.) (1933–1967). *Diodorus of Sicily / Diodorus Siculus,* 12 volumes. Cambridge: Harvard University Press.

Onyewuenyi, Innocent. (1993). *The African Origin of Greek Philosophy: An Exercise in Afrocentrism.* Nsukka, Nigeria: University of Nigeria Press.

Pawley, A. and M. Ross. (1993). "Austronesian historical linguistics and culture history," *Annual Review of Anthropology,* 22, 425–459.

Perry, Rufus L. (1893). *The Cushite or Descendants of Ham.* Springfield, Massachusetts: Willey.

Pfouma, Oscar. (1993). O*L'abeille royale,* CarbetL *Revue Martinique de Sciences Humaines et de Litterature,* no.6, 98–105.

Robins, R. H. (1974). *General Linguistics.* Bloomington: Indiana State University Press.

Ruhlen, M. (1994). *The Origin of Language.* New York: John Wiley & Sons, Inc.

Senghor, L. S. (1961). "Negritude and African Socialism," *African Affairs,* 2, 20–25.

Snowden, Frank M. (1983). *Before Color Prejudice: The Ancient View of Blacks.* Cambridge: Harvard University Press.

———. (1970). *Blacks in Antiquity: Ethiopians in the Greco-Roman Experience.* Cambridge: Harvard University Press.

Snowden, Frank M. (1987). *Blacks in the Ancient Greece and Roman World: An Introduction to the Exhibit.* Washington, D.C.: Howard University Libraries.

Tiffany, John. (2004). "The Racial Makeup of the Original Egyptians,"*Barnes Review,* (January/February) 5–13.

Toukara, B. (1989). "Problematique du comparatisme, egyptien ancien/langues africaines (Wolof)," *Présence Africaine,* No.149/150, 313–320.

Van Serima, Ivan, (ed.) (1995). *Nile Valley Civiulizations, Proceedings of the Nile Valley Conference.* New Brunswick: Journal of African Civilizations.

———. (ed.) (1989). *Egypt Revisited.* New Brunswick: Transaction Press.

———. (ed.) (1994). *Egypt, Child of Africa.* New Brunswick: Transaction Press.

Van Sertima, Ivan and Larry Obadele Williams, (eds.) (1986) *Great African Thinkers, Vol. 1: Cheikh Anta Diop.* New Brunswick: Transaction Press.

Volney, Constantine, F. (1913). *Travels Through Syria and Egypt.* London: G. G. J. and James Robinson.

Wauthier, Claude. (1964). *L'Afrique des Africaines.* Paris: Ed. de Seuil.

Wharton, E. R. (1974). *Etymological Lexicon of Classical Greek.* Chicago: Ares Publishers.

Williams, B. (1987). *The A-Group Royal Cemetery at Qustul: Cemetery L.* Chicago: Oriental Institute, University of Chicago Press.

Williams, Chancellor. (1976). *The Destruction of Black Civilization: Great Issues of a Race from 4500 B.C. to 2000 A.D.* Chicago: Third World Press.

Williams, Clarence. (2004). *L'Impossible Retour.* Paris: Karthala.

George W. Williams. (1968). *History of the Negro Race in America from 1619 to 1880 . . . and an Historical sketch of Africa.* New York: Bergman.

Winters, Clyde Ahmad. (1985). "The Indus Valley Writing and related Scripts of the 3rd Millennium B.C.," *India Past and Present* 2, No. 1, 13–19.

———. (2002). "Ancient Afrocentric History and the Genetic Model," in M. Asante and Ama Mazama (eds.), *Egypt v. Greece in the American Academy.* Chicago: African American Images, pp. 121–164.

———. (1989). "Cheikh Anta Diop et le dechiffrement de l'ecriture meroitique," *Carbet: Revue Martinique de Sciences Humaines et de Litterature,* 8–152.

———. (1989). *"Review of* Dr. Asko Parpolas' 'The Coming of the Aryans'," *International Journal of Dravidian Linguistics* 18, 2, 98–127.

———. (1994). "Afrocentrism: A valid Frame of References," *Journal of Black Studies* 25, 2, 170–190.

Zewde, Bahru. (2002). *Pioneers of Change in Ethiopia.* Athens: Ohio University Press.

INDEX